Doldrum Bay

Hilary Fannin

Methuen Drama

Published by Methuen 2003

1 3 5 7 9 10 8 6 4 2

First published in 2003 by
Methuen Publishing Limited,
215 Vauxhall Bridge Road,
London SW1V 1EJ

Methuen Publishing Limited Reg. No. 3543167

A CIP catalogue record is available from the British Library

ISBN 0 413 77362 0

Typeset by SX Composing DTP, Rayleigh, Essex
Printed and bound in Great Britain by
Cox & Wyman Ltd, Reading, Berkshire

Caution

The Abbey Theatre

Doldrum Bay

By Hilary Fannin

The Abbey Theatre gratefully acknowledges the financial
support from the Arts Council/An Chomhairle Ealaíon

New Writing in the Abbey Theatre

Since its foundation in 1904, the Abbey Theatre has been the cradle of new writing and drama in Ireland for successive generations of Irish playwrights. From Synge and O'Casey, to playwrights at the cutting edge of contemporary Irish theatre, developing and producing new plays remain at the very core of the Abbey Theatre's artistic policy. Over the last year, as part of its continuing commitment to the nurturing and development of new writing, the Abbey has commissioned fourteen new plays for both the Abbey and Peacock Theatres.

The Abbey's Literary Department continually seeks out, encourages and develops the best of new Irish and international playwriting. Its Seeding Project (made possible by financial assistance from the Calouste Gulbenkian Foundation) in which emerging playwrights are invited to develop a project or play using the full resources of the Literary Department, has currently twelve projects in development – with plans to initiate more in 2004. Along with its full schedule of play readings and workshops, the Literary Department assesses and responds to over three hundred unsolicited scripts a year, and has just completed its first series of dramaturgical workshops, entitled PlayTalk, which offer the participants the opportunity to further their potential as playwrights.

As part of the Abbey's commitment to the promotion of Irish writing, new plays continue to be published as part of the Abbey Theatre Playscript Series and Volume Three of **New Plays from the Abbey Theatre** has been recently published.

Doldrum Bay

by Hilary Fannin

Doldrum Bay by Hilary Fannin was first performed at the Peacock Theatre on 7 May 2003. Press night was 13 May 2003.

The play is set on a peninsula, in the present.

There will be one interval of 15 minutes

Cast in order of Appearance

Magda	Ali White
Francis	Risteárd Cooper
Chick	Owen Roe
Java	Ruth Negga
Louise	Karen Ardiff
Mousey	Darragh Kelly
Director	Mark Lambert
Set Design	Jamie Vartan
Costume Design	Catherine Fay
Lighting Designer	Tina MacHugh
Sound Designer	Ivan Birthistle
Voice Director	Andrea Ainsworth
Stage Director	John Stapleton
Assistant Stage Manager	Stephen Dempsey
Casting Director	Marie Kelly
Set	Abbey Theatre Workshop
Costumes	Abbey Theatre Wardrobe Department
Director of the Peacock	Ali Curran

Please note that the text of the play which appears in this volume may be changed during the rehearsal process and appear in a slightly altered form in performance.

Hilary Fannin *Writer*

Hilary Fannin was born in Dublin and has worked as an actor throughout the eighties and nineties. Her plays include **Mackerel Sky,** Bush Theatre, London, **Sleeping Around,** a collaboration with Mark Ravenhill and others, Donmar Warehouse, London and for BBC Radio 4, **Time It Was, Red Feathers** and **Dear Exile**.

Mark Lambert *Director*

Mark is an Associate Director of the Abbey Theatre. Recent productions include **The Hunt for Red Willie, The Memory of Water** and **Lovers at Versailles** at the Abbey and Peacock Theatres. He recently directed **Baldi,** a six part BBC radio series and **The Memory of Water** at the Lyric Theatre. Other directing work includes **The Grapes of Wrath** for Storytellers, **Una Pooka,** Tricycle, London and numerous productions at the Royal Lyceum Theatre, Edinburgh. Performances at the Abbey and Peacock Theatres include **Ariel, The Gigli Concert, Observe the Sons of Ulster Marching towards the Somme** and **Barbaric Comedies** for which he received an Irish Times/ESB nomination. At the Gate Theatre he performed in **Molly Sweeney, Art, The Three Sisters** and **A Month in the Country**. In England he performed at the West End in **Juno and the Paycock,** Albery Theatre for which he was nominated for an Olivier Award for his Joxer, **Dancing at Lughnasa** and **The Memory of Water**. Other work includes productions at the RSC, Royal Court, Hampstead, Bush and Young Vic Theatres. Television credits include **Cracker, Dalziel and Pascoe, Frost, Bloody Sunday, No Tears, Sharpe's Rifles, Casualty, Vanity Fair, Fair City, Bottom, Fergus' Wedding** and **The Young Ones**. Films include **A Prayer for the Dying, Durango, Jude, Borstal Boy** and **Evelyn** and he will soon be seen in **Chasing the Dragon, Dark Eagle** and **Rosemary and Thyme** on ITV.

Jamie Vartan *Designer*

Jamie trained at Central Saint Martin's School of Art and Design, London. He was awarded an Arts Council Bursary to work at Nottingham Playhouse where he designed several productions. Previous work at the Abbey and Peacock Theatres includes **The Playboy of the Western World, The Hostage, A Little Like Paradise, Sour Grapes, Making History, Mrs Warren's Profession** (nomination for Irish Times Theatre Awards Best Production), **The Hunt for Red Willie** and **Blackwater Angel.** He was involved for three years as Designer and Artist-in-Residence with the David Glass Ensemble on **The Lost Child Trilogy,** which has included residencies involving workshops, research and new devised productions in Vietnam, Indonesia, China, the Philippines and Colombia. The Trilogy was later presented at the Young Vic. His work on **The Hansel Gretel Machine** (part one of the Trilogy) was selected for the 1999 Prague Quadrennial Theatre Design Exhibition. Other recent theatre work includes **Because it's There,** Nottingham Playhouse and **The Memory of Water,** Lyric Theatre, Belfast. Opera includes **La Traviata,** Malmo Musikteater, Sweden, **A Village Romeo and Juliet,** Teatro Lirico dei Cagliari, Sardinia, **The Dwarf,** Teatro Cumunale, Florence and Teatregio, Turin and currently, **La Statira,** Teatro San Carlo, Naples. Design for dance with choreographer Darshan Singh Bhuller includes **Recall,** Linbury Studio, Royal Opera House and on tour, a new production, **Requiem** for Phoenix Dance Company at Sadlers Wells and UK tour.

Catherine Fay *Costume Designer*

Catherine is a graduate of the National College of Art and Design. She is the costume designer for Bedrock Theatre Company. She has designed **Chair** for Operating Theatre Company, **On Such as We** and **Henry IV Part 1** (for which she received an Irish Times/ESB nomination) at the Peacock Theatre. She recently designed **Antigone** and **Women in Arms** for Storytellers Theatre Company. Other productions include **Lessness** for Gare St Lazare Players performed during the Kilkenny Festival and at The National Theatre in London and **The Massacre @ Paris** for Bedrock.

Tina MacHugh *Lighting Designer*

Previous designs at the Abbey and Peacock Theatres include **The Wexford Trilogy, The Last Ones, Hedda Gabler, The Playboy of the Western World** and **The Hunt for Red Willie**. Other theatre work includes **The Book of Evidence**, Kilkenny Festival, **Shoot the Crow**, Druid Theatre, **Midden, The Whisperers**, Rough Magic Theatre Company, **Sharon's Grave**, Gate Theatre, **A Doll's House, Mother Courage** and **The House of Bernarda Alba**, Shared Experience Theatre, **The Tempest, Love in a Wood, The Comedy of Errors, Ghosts, Henry VI** and **Shadows**, Royal Shakespeare Company, **Rutherford & Son, The Machine Wreckers**, and **Guiding Star**, Royal National Theatre, **Yard Gal**, Royal Court Theatre, **Nixon's Nixon**, Comedy Theatre, **Our Father**, Almeida Theatre and **Spoonface Steinberg**, New Ambassadors Theatre. Tina was nominated for an Olivier Award for her work on **Ghosts** and **Rutherford & Son**. Opera includes **Il Re Pastore**, Opera North, **The Juniper Tree**, Munich Biennale/Almeida Opera Festival, **Idomeneo** and **The Tales of Hoffman**, De Vlaamse Opera, Antwerp and **Der Rosenkavalier**, Scottish Opera. Dance includes work with Rambert Dance Company, DV8, Adventures in Motion Pictures, English National Ballet, London Contemporary Dance Company and Royal Danish Ballet.

Ivan Birthistle *Sound Designer*

Ivan's sound design includes **Ladies and Gents** by Semper Fi, **24 Hours of Dance**, Project, **Slaughter** and **Feint**, Pan Pan Festival, Arthouse, **Massacre @ Paris**, Bedrock Productions and **Butterflies**, Dublin Fringe Festival and Berlin.

Karen Ardiff *Louise*

Karen was born in Dublin and graduated from the Samuel Beckett Centre in TCD. Previous appearances for the Abbey and Peacock Theatres include **Love in the Title** (Abbey international tour, for which she won the ESB/Irish Times Best Actress Award), **Caoineadh Airt Uí Laoghaire, Cúirt an Mheán Óiche** (Peacock and national tour), **Judas of the Gallarus, The Rivals, Tarry Flynn** (Abbey and Royal National Theatre), **The Marriage of Figaro, The Well Of The Saints** (Abbey and Edinburgh tour), **Good Evening Mr.Collins** (Peacock and national tour) and **The Crucible**. Karen has worked with theatre companies across Ireland in productions which include **Kvetch** (Kilkenny Arts Festival), **How I Learned To Drive** (Lyric Belfast), **The Cherry Orchard, A Month in the Country** and **The Seagull** (Gate), **Silas Marner** (Storytellers), **To** (Bickerstaffe), **The Ashfire** (Pigsback) and international tours with the English Shakespeare Company in **The Winter's Tale** and **Coriolanus**. For Guna Nua, Karen appeared in **The Importance of Being Earnest** (Civic Theatre, Tallaght) and most recently in Guna Nua's Production of **Taste**, written and directed by David Parnell, at Andrews Lane Theatre. Film and television includes **Evelyn, Sinners** (BBC/RTE), **Fergus' Wedding** (RTE), **This Is My Father, Ballykissangel** (BBC/RTE) and **Glenroe** (RTE). Karen has also appeared in numerous RTE and BBC radio drama productions including **Crazy Dog Audio** (RTE), **The Monotonous Life of Little Miss P** (BBCNI), **Three Sisters** (RTE), **Gone But Forgotten** (RTE), **Parachutes** (BBCNI), **I Do Not Like Thee Dr. Fell** (RTE) and Gerard Stembridge's **Daisy The Cow Who Talked** (RTE).

Risteárd Cooper *Francis*

Risteárd's previous appearances at the Abbey Theatre include **Moses Rock** and Frank McGuinness' **The Bird Sanctuary**. He lived in America for several years where he worked with the Ensemble Studio Theatre and the Irish Rep in New York, appearing in numerous productions including **Talking Back, Juno and The Paycock** and **Same Old Moon** and with Steppenwolf Theatre Company, Chicago he played Mickey in the American premiere of **Mojo** by Jez Butterworth. At the GateTheatre Risteárd appeared in **Cyrano De Bergerac, Arcadia, An Ideal Husband, Blithe Spirit, See You Next Tuesday** and most recently **Eccentricities of a Nightingale** by Tennessee Williams. Other theatre work includes **A Little Like Drowning**, Druid Theatre Company, **Buffalo Bill Has Gone to Alaska**, Pigsback, **Blood Brothers**, Olympia Theatre and **A Slice of Saturday Night** at Andrews Lane. He also toured Ireland and the US in productions of **Bedtime Story, End of the Beginning** and **The Shadow of a Gunman**, all directed by Shivaun O'Casey. Risteárd is one third of comedy team **Après Match** which has, apart from its work on RTE, toured all over Ireland enjoying runs in Vicar St, The Gaiety, Cork Opera House and at last year's Galway Arts Festival. Their third video, **Tired and Emotional**, went double platinum and reached No. 1 in the Irish charts at the end of 2002. Risteárd is a graduate of the acting programme at the Samuel Beckett Centre, Trinity College.

Darragh Kelly *Mousey*

Darragh's previous performances at the Abbey and Peacock Theatres include **All My Sons, Philadelphia Here I Come!, Angels In America, Give Me Your Answer Do!, The Colleen Bawn** and **The Importance of Being Earnest**. Other work includes **Three Days of Rain, Digging for Fire, Way of the World, Northern Star, School For Scandal** and **Hidden Charges,** Rough Magic and **Our Father,** Almeida. Television credits include **Ballykissangel, Double Carpet, Paths to Freedom** and **Cape Random.** Films include **Nora, Connemara, The General,** and **Veronica Guerin,** soon to be released.

Ruth Negga *Java*

Ruth graduated with a Bachelor in Acting Studies from the Samuel Beckett Centre, Trinity College Dublin last November. Her appearances at the Abbey and Peacock Theatres include **Lolita** (in association with The Corn Exchange) and **Sons and Daughters**. Other work includes **Súile Eile** with Fluxus Dance Company and **Amy and Her Sister Martina** for Corcadorca Theatre company.

Owen Roe *Chick*

Owen's most recent appearances at the Abbey and Peacock Theatres were as Fluther Good in **The Plough and Stars** and The Irish Man in **The Gigli Concert** both directed by Ben Barnes. Owen also appeared as Oscar in **Tartuffe,** John Proctor in **The Crucible,** The Director in **Six Characters in Search of an Author, The Corsican Brothers, The Mai, Sheep's Milk on the Boil, Moses Rock, Prayers of Sherkin** and Eddie in **One Last White Horse.** He also performed in **Shadow of a Gunman** as Seamus Sheils, **Great Expectations, The Cherry Orchard** and **Romeo and Juliet** at the Gate Theatre. Owen was nominated Best Actor for an Irish Times/ESB Theatre Award as Neils Bohr in the Irish premiere of Michael Frayn's **Copenhagen** directed by Lynne Parker at Project. Television credits include Paul Dooley in **Ballykissangel** (BBC), Kevin Flaherty in **The Ambassador, The Broker's Man** (ITV), **Making the Cut, DDU, The Governor, Scarlett, The Treaty** and **Soft Sand, Blue Sea** and the BBC/RTE drama series **Anytime Now.** Film credits include **When the Sky Falls, Frankie Starlight, Undercurrent,** Arthur Griffith in Neil Jordan's **Michael Collins** and Henderson in John Crowley's **Intermission.**

Ali White *Magda*

Ali trained at the Gaiety School of Acting. Previous performances at the Abbey and Peacock Theatres include **Dancing at Lughnasa, Translations, Philadelphia, Here I Come!** , **The Trojan Women, The House** and **Closer.** Other theatre work includes **The School for Scandal, Northern Star, Lady Windermere's Fan** and **Love and a Bottle** (Time Out Award) for Rough Magic, **Aristocrats, The Double Dealer** and **A Midsummer Night's Dream** at the Gate Theatre, **Play, Come and Go, Catastrophe,** Gate Theatre and at the Barbican Theatre, London as part of the Beckett Festival, **Silas Marner** and **Hard Times** for Storytellers, **Cheapside** for Druid Theatre Company, **Factory Girls** for Bickerstaffe and two seasons at the Lyric Theatre, Belfast. Outside Ireland she has appeared in **The Steward of Christendom,** Out of Joint, **The Silver Tassie,** Almeida, **Pygmies in the Ruins,** Royal Court Theatre, **The Importance of Being Earnest,** West Yorkshire Playhouse and **Playhouse Creatures** at the Old Vic. Film and television includes **When Brendan Met Trudy** , **A Love Divided, With or Without You** , **The Ambassador** and **Flush.** Ali is a frequent performer on RTE Radio drama and BBC Radio Ulster. Last year Ali's first writing project, **Any Time Now,** a six part drama series, was produced by Comet Films for RTE and BBC television.

The Abbey Theatre

Doldrum Bay

In memory of my father Bob Fannin

Doldrum Bay premièred at the Peacock stage of the Abbey Theatre, Dublin, on 7 May 2003. The cast was as follows:

Magda	Ali White
Francis	Risteárd Cooper
Louise	Karen Ardiff
Chick	Owen Roe
Java	Ruth Negga
Mousey	Darragh Kelly

Director Mark Lambert
Set Designer Jamie Vartan
Costume Designer Catherine Fay
Lighting Designer Tina MacHugh
Sound Designer Ivan Birthistle

Characters

Magda, *late thirties / early forties*
Francis, *late thirties / early forties*
Louise, *late thirties / early forties*
Chick, *late thirties / early forties*
Java, *early twenties*
Mousey, *late thirties / early forties*

Act One

Scene One

A beach, rocky, enclosed. A raised area serves as a large bed. On the bed, electronic equipment, mobile phone, hand-held camera. Video player/screen faces bed. Video is playing, audible not visible. Traffic sounds are constant background to video footage.

Video.

Francis   One, one, two, one. Right: research, novel. Subject: taxi driver, middle-aged male. Would you call yourself middle-aged?

Driver   I'd call myself Pocahontas if it got the traffic moving.

Francis   Right, very good. Couple of questions, as I say, research for a novel I'm writing.

Driver   Yep.

Francis   I'm a writer, you see. I'm writing a novel.

Driver   So you said. What's it about?

Francis   Religion. Sex, actually. Religion and sex.

Driver   Tell you about religion: my daughter was confirmed last Friday. I sat in a church for two hours, listening to a man in a paper hat telling me fairy stories. I'm thinking it's alright for you, pal, with your dressy up box and your jiggery-pokery, you don't open your own bills.

Magda *enters. She is dressed for outdoors. As she listens she moves around, removes coat etc. She is at home.*

Driver   Nobody is listening. The kids are adding up how much they'll make out of the day. The holy spirit does a turn. And we say a prayer to the unborn. To all those that never saw the light of day.

My wife and I have three kids. The middle one, Martin, is an artist. He is the happiest man I know. I'm thinking, I see the point now, he is the fucking point.

Magda *is still. She focuses on the video.*

Driver   Month ago my wife finds out she's pregnant. She tells me what we're doing about it. We go to London make a weekend of it, see *Les Mis*, fantastic. Back home Sunday night, get a take-away, no more said about it. My daughter's swimming through a crocodile-infested moat on the P.S.2, I say to her, what name are you taking for the confirmation? Amber, she says. I don't remember a Saint Amber, I say. So, she says, I like it. That's what I'm having. Wife says, Amber is a great name. So now we are all hunky-dory.

Francis   Right, so…?

Francis *enters. He has just showered.*

Driver   Later my wife says to me it wasn't a baby yet, it was cells, but if it had been a girl I would have called her Amber. She turns over she goes to sleep. And I'm lying there. I'm thinking, they're right, it doesn't fuckin' matter any more.
It doesn't fucking matter. Lauren Mary Amber.

Francis   Hello. (*About the video*) Research.

Driver   What the fuck does that mean? What in the name of suffering Jesus are we? What was the question? I can't remember the question.

End of video. Beat. **Magda** *stays looking at the screen.*

Francis   Interviewed him in his taxi.

Magda   It's moving.

Francis   The taxi wasn't.

Magda   It's sad.

Francis   Is it? Good. I'll use him.

Beat. **Francis** *clears up electronic equipment.* **Magda** *turns on answering machine.*

Francis   My agent rang.

Magda   Yeah?

Francis   Lot of excitement apparently.

Magda   Good.

Francis   She said it's hot.

Answering Machine   *Magda, awful news. Call me, we need to talk about a retrospective.*

Magda   Hot?

Francis   Contemporary.

Answering Machine   *Magda, is he dead yet? /*

Magda   Terrific.

Answering Machine   *Everyone else is. Who's left?*

Francis   Sex and God, she said you basically can't beat sex and . . .

Answering Machine   *Have you thought about an obit?*

Francis   . . . God in a *contemporaneous* novel.

Answering Machine   *Best if you telephone me.*

Magda   Great. Good. Good. Good. That's really good.

Francis   How was he?

Magda   Same.

Francis   Same, yeah?

Magda   They said they'd keep the fluids going, keep the morphine / going

Francis   Good. Chick rang by the way.

Magda   Have you got a cigarette?

Francis   He sounds pretty stressed.

Magda (*cigarette*)   Francis? Cigarette?

Francis   No. He needs to meet up with me some bloody crisis or other.

Magda   So, are you going to?

Francis   What?

Magda   Meet?

Francis   Yes.

Beat.

Shortly.

Magda   Oh.

Francis   Filmic, that was the other thing. She also said the work was very filmic.

Magda   Who said?

Francis   Jules. My agent. She said the work was potentially very filmic. Of course, she wants a fucking draft / yesterday.

Magda   Right.

Francis   I said you can't rush this.

Magda   Sure.

Francis   Faith. She said. Desire. Wow. Breakdown of traditional / mores. Love it.

Magda   Right.

Francis   I *buy* that world. I buy into your world. She said. Now is that a fucking endorsement? / Or is that an endorsement?

Magda   It's . . . great /

Francis   I *buy* your world.

Magda   Great. Really.

Francis   Best move I ever made. What are you doing?

Magda   Looking for a cigarette.

Francis   You've given up.

Magda   Right. Great.

Francis   Like I say, I'm really feeling it was the right move.

Magda   What move was that?

Francis   Once you feel that imperative, to create something, something unadulterated, something /

Magda   Art?

Beat.

Francis   Yes.

Magda   Good. Do you have one?

Francis   No.

Beat.

Magda   I told them I didn't want any more intervention.

Francis   Sorry?

Magda   He'll drown. The fluid in his chest will fill up his lungs and he'll drown. Ironic.

Francis   What?

Magda   He'll drown.

Francis   Jesus / Magda.

Magda   Fine / I'm fine.

Francis   I'm sorry.

Magda   They said I should talk to him.

Francis   Can he hear you?

Magda   I don't know.
I don't know.
I keep thinking he's thirsty. His tongue is black. They can't give him anything to drink, just little wet sticks they roll around his mouth like a promise.

Francis   Right. Nice.

Magda   What?

Francis   No, no. Nothing.

Magda   I said don't try to bring him back.

Francis   No.

Magda   I don't want another year scraping his food into the dog dish. The last time I picked him up I thought his skin would come off in my hands.

Beat.

Francis   I need to get going. Chick will be getting anxious.

Pause. She watches him dress.

Magda   I don't know what to say to him.

Francis   He probably can't / hear you.

Magda   She told me to touch him. Hold his hand or something.

Francis   Who?

Magda   The nun.

Francis   What nun?

Magda   Comfort.

Francis   Comfort?

Magda   They bring comfort.

Francis   Who?

Magda   Religious people. Nuns. Goretti said /

Francis   Goretti?

Magda   That the kingdom of God has many mansions
and that a place was being prepared for him. That helped
me.

Francis   Goretti?

Magda   I found that reassuring. Comforting.

Francis   It's language, Magda. It's only language.

Magda   She sits with him. She touches him. I can't do
that.

Francis   He'd hate that.

Magda   I told her he wasn't a religious man, he wouldn't
want ritual, he wouldn't want purification or whatever it is
they do. She said Jesus was preparing a place and when it
was time /

Francis   When it was time, what?

Magda   I don't know. I don't know what.

Francis   Goretti! Don't

Magda   I don't remember giving up smoking.

Francis   Don't get caught up in / hocus-fucking-pocus.

Magda   I'm not getting caught up in anything /

Francis   Nuns! You're a fucking heathen.

Magda   Am I?

Francis   'Am I?' Jesus, Magda, you had sex with me in a
confessional.

Magda   We were young.

Francis   We were making a statement.

Magda   You were making a statement. I was being agreeable.

Francis   Very.

Magda   I need to feed her. What time is it?

Francis   You should go to bed.

Magda   Goretti asked if there was anyone else. Any other family that needed to be informed. I said, there's his dog. He's close to his dog. He loves the dog. 'Would you rather a bit of chicken?' 'Would you prefer to sit over there?' It's perverse. 'How are you feeling?' She's a dog. What does he think, she's going to turn around and tell him she's depressed?

Francis   You need sleep. I'll feed her on my way to meet Chick.

Magda   What's wrong with him?

Francis   He's about to be fired.
Style thing. His ideas are dated. His dress sense is offensive. He's a middle-aged pedant working with a bunch of illiterates in shorts. I fuckin' warned him. He should have got out when I did.

Magda   Poor Chick.
Maybe he'll write a novel too.

Francis   Sorry?

Magda   You look nice.

Francis   This book is not some Mickey Mou . . . This is my work Magda, this is my story, my contribution to the fucking firmament Magda. Okay?

Magda   Sure

Francis   My agent . . .

Magda   Jules.

Francis   Jules, yes. Jules said this book will blast dogma off the shelves / teach us to live the the the . . . animal, the instinctual.

Magda   Animal.

Francis   Magda!

Magda   Give me a cigarette.

Francis   I don't have a cigarette.

Magda   Stay!

Pause. She watches him, her attention making him uncomfortable.

So what's it about?

Beat.

Francis   You know what it's about.

Magda   God and sex?

Francis   God, sex, identity /

Magda   Did you write about me?

Francis   No.

Magda   Did you write about me in the confessional?

Francis   No, that's private.

Beat.

Magda   I wasn't just being agreeable.

Francis   I know you weren't just being agreeable.

Beat.

I'm sorry. I'm sorry you have to go through this. If there's something you / want me . . .

Magda   There is nothing you can do.

Francis   Right.

Magda   It's taking so long. What's he hanging on for? What does he want?

Francis (*now dressed*)   Are you going back in tonight?

Magda   Yes.

Francis   I spoke to that 'Artoclysm' woman. She needs his signature on some of his prints before / he . . .

Magda   Right.

Francis   Her tone was appropriately reverential.

Magda   I wish she'd fuck off. I wish they'd all fuck off.

Francis   Tell them. I'll tell them.

Magda   I can't.

Francis   Do you want me to drop by, feed the dog?

Magda   You can try. She won't come out. She won't leave the studio. She's waiting for him to come back.

Francis   She'll be OK.

Magda   I don't think so. She's been fucked up all her life, why should now be any different?

Francis   I'll feed her.

Magda   Sure.

Beat.

Will you be long?

Francis   Not very.

Beat.

Goodbye.

Beat.

Magda? Goodbye.

Magda   See ya.

Exit **Francis**. **Magda** *sits. After a moment she turns on video.*

    Driver   I ask myself, what have I done? What will I leave behind? What have I done? Anything? What was the question? I've forgotten the question.

Scene Two

Beach. Mellow electronic music. There are two bar stools, the seats resembling open shells.

Java, *a young woman dressed as a mermaid, moves around setting up drinks.*

Enter **Francis**.

Downstage, **Chick** *struggles to sit on one of the bar stools.* **Francis** *joins* **Chick**.

Chick   Style police check you for labels at the door?

Francis   No.

Chick   Checked *me*. Told me to take *off* my tie. Lowered the tone.

Francis   Why don't you sit down?

Chick   I'm trying to. (*Sitting, looking around.*) What is this place anyway?

Francis   It's conceptual.

Chick   What's the concept?

Francis   Fish.

Chick   Fish? Terrific.

Java *approaches with oxygen mask / cylinder on wheels.*

Chick   What's she doing? Scuba diving?

Java (*to* **Chick**)   Would you gentlemen like to try the oxygen?

Chick   No.

Java   It's a speciality of the house.

Francis (*to* **Java**)   Thanks.

Java   Can I get you guys the wine list?

Francis   Terrific.

Java *gives mask to* **Francis**, *who places it over his face and breathes*. **Java** *goes*.

Chick   You paying for that stuff?

Francis   It's air; of course I pay for it.

Pause. **Chick** *watches* **Francis** *breathe*. **Francis** *breathes doggedly. Eventually* . . .

Chick   So. How's the novel?

Francis   Treatment. It's never a good idea to talk about art.

Chick   Is it not?

Java *returns with the wine list*.

Francis   However, as you asked nicely.
(*To* **Java**.) Thank you.
My novel is a fucking phenomenon. Huge excitement.
(*To* **Java**.) Sorry.

Java   Take your time.

Francis   God and sex. I'm looking at how desire can secularise a nation.

Chick   Right. It's a comedy then?

Francis   Publisher's screaming for a draft.

Java   May I recommend the Santa Rita Reserva. It's a frisky little Chilean.

Francis   A frisky little Chilean? Wonderful. Will you be joining us?

Java   Thanks.

She goes to get wine. Beat.

Chick   Frisky little Chilean?

Francis   Fuck it.

Chick   So. How's the novel?

Francis   Challenging.

Chick   Bit like our pre-packed smorgasbord campaign?

Francis   Not even remotely.

Chick   Oh.

Francis   My agent's very /

Chick   Inexperienced /

Francis   Excited. She says it's hot.

Chick   Yeah?

Francis   Filmic. She mentioned filmic. Twice.

Chick   Great.

Francis   Still have to write the fuckin' thing.

Java *returns with bottle.*

Francis   Filmic, in her opinion, did I mention that?

Java   Taste?

Francis   I'm sure it's perfect.
(*Tasting.*) Fantastic. Join us.

Java (*removing oxygen cylinder*)   Let me just get this.

Chick   Careful now with that thing. You never know when it might come in handy.

Java *begins to remove oxygen.*

Francis (*to* **Chick**)   What of the tawdry world of toilet paper advertising?

Chick   That was one of my better campaigns.

Francis   Sadly.

Chick (*to* **Java**)   I was the one who thought of naming toilet paper after the French Impressionists.

Java   It's very brave of you to admit it.

Chick (*to* **Java**)   It was a fantastic campaign. It changed something purely functionary into something desirable. It was a pastel revolution. It blurred the line between art and /

Java   Right. What is it you do?

Chick   Advertising.

Java *goes.*

Francis (*appreciatively*)   Jesus.

Chick   Things are bad.

Francis   Yeah?

Chick   We got a new receptionist.

Francis   Oh yeah?

Chick   I'm casually draped over her frosted-glass block, introducing myself. She asks me if I need a chair.

Francis   Shit.

Chick   I'm out.
I refuse to be fired by someone in three-quarter-length trousers. Teenage creatives with their fucking montages and retro soundtracks. What happened to dancing bears and ladies on bonnets? Tits? Tits don't sell anything any more; we are all beyond gender, apparently.

Francis   Cheers.

Chick   Cheers. They gave me haemorrhoids.

Francis   What?

Chick   Eight-by-fours of the interiors of people's arseholes sellotaped around the office.

Francis   Jesus.

Chick   The rest of the team have gone snowboarding in Reykjavik. They got party packs – seaweed massage oil and edible condoms. I got /

Francis   Haemorrhoids.

Chick   Right. Nobody else would touch them. I went to the new MD, who must be getting on for twelve. I said, I'm pretty experienced at this team-building business, if you'd like me to join you in Iceland. He said, we need someone to stay on top of the /

Francis   Piles.

Chick   Right. I'm building my launch campaign around the cream's unique unisex appeal.

Francis   Where did she go?

Chick   A tincture of menthol for the boys, a splash of lavender for the girls. Offering all-day relief with built-in freshness and guaranteed shrinkage.

Francis   Yeah?

Chick   I'm toying with the name 'Bum's rush – it'll get you in the end.'

Pause. **Francis** *looks at him.*

Didn't think so.

Beat.

They want the car back.

Francis (*looking at* **Java**)   Phenomenal fucking tail fin.

Chick   They've offered me a bicycle. Said it's a funkier image for the company. I told them I don't want a bicycle. I like my car, I'm too old for a bicycle. They offered me a skateboard. You don't need to be a rocket scientist to see which way the wind is blowing.

Francis   No.

Chick   Of course, I *can't* give back the car, can I? Louise has glued fridge magnets all over the dash. 'We live our life through Jesus.' I'm like a moving shrine.

Francis   Lost it again, has she?

Chick   'We live our life through Jesus', my bollix, I said to her. Jesus isn't paying for the Club Med, the decking, the leisure centre, the driving range, the people carrier, the Grecian-tiled downstairs WC, the health centre, the spa, the anniversary marquee, the appliance garage.

Francis   No.

Chick   My job, I tried to explain to her, is to covet, steal, and exploit. That, she says, lying on the Dalmation bedspread which gives me a migraine, scraping her nail polish off one puffy little hand with the other puffy little hand, is the problem. That is it exactly.

He drinks, pours another.

Marriage!

Francis/Chick (*in-joke*)   Terms and conditions apply.

Francis *gestures for* **Java**.

Chick   'Bum's rush – your end is our beginning.'

Francis   No.

Java *arrives.*

Francis   Hi. We may need another.

Java   Cool.

She goes. They drink.

Francis   Jesus, she is /

Chick   How's Jakey?

Francis   Still dying. He has a tumour.

Chick   Size of a cauliflower, right?

Francis   I've no idea.

Chick   They usually are, or a grapefruit. Quite popular, those two sizes. How's Magda taking it?

Francis   Hard to tell.

Chick   Paintings?

Francis   Magda has some. Lot of the later stuff was bartered for sex or drink.

Chick   End of an era.

Francis   He wasn't that good.

Chick   He was though. Gas man, Jakey. He didn't give a flying fuck, did he?

Jakey.

Francis   Jakey.

Pause. They both drink, **Chick** *too quickly. After a hesitation he picks up bottle and pours himself another glass.*

Chick   I'm under pressure.

Francis   I know.

Chick   You *don't* know. You do not know the fucking pressure I am under. Work, Louise, Dessie.

Francis   What about Dessie?

Chick   He lost the plot in Iowa. The order are calling him back.

Francis   Dessie?

Chick   Walked out on his parish. Got himself a job as a demonstration bunny in Wal-Mart.

Francis   Dessie? Is a demonstration bunny in Wal-Mart?

Chick   Consecrating the Liebfraumilch. He's very popular. The local football team made him their mascot.

Francis   Dessie? Fuckin' hell.

Chick   I need this like a hole in the head.

Francis   What? Dessie in a bunny suit?

Chick   I got a phone call from a priest called Bamber. He's being sent out to Iowa to bring Dessie home. Asks me if I want to join him. I say I could think of more entertaining ways to spend an afternoon than being strapped into an empty tumble-dryer three thousand feet up getting deep-vein thrombosis. Bamber says it's serious. The normally sedate Iowan parishioners are deeply pissed off. Anyway, Bamber asks me to meet him at the airport, have a chat, give him some extenuating for Dessie's little escapade.

Francis   Poor bastard.

Chick   Been coming for years. He's the loneliest man on the planet, Dessie. Iowa? For fuck's sake.

Francis   Rabbit?

Chick   You know the man has never had a ride? I feel like Don fuckin' Juan beside him / and I'm not.

Francis   And you're not.

Chick   I'm about to leave to go and meet Bamber when Louise's tinkly little phone rings again. It rings to the tune of 'Frère Jacques', drives me up the wall. I'm trying to dive on it before it tells me to 'dormez-vous'. I grab the receiver, which incidentally is a plastic representation of one of the many bridges of Bruges. She won it in a painting competition; second prize was two of them. I grab the receiver and a voice says . . .

Java *returns with second bottle.*

Francis   What's your name?

Java   Java.

Chick (*quietly*)   Christ.

Francis   Fantastic, Java. Get yourself a glass.

She goes.

(*To* **Chick**.) And a voice says?

Chick   Mousey.

Francis (*calling*) Java.
(*To* **Chick**,) What?

Chick   Mousey.

Java (*returning*)   Yeah?

Francis   It's a beautiful name.

Java   Thanks.

She leaves.

Chick   Mousey. Remember Mousey? We were in school with him. Ugly bastard, fuck-all chin. Sat beside that bloke with the harelip.

Francis   Goo.

Chick   Goo. Right. Poor cunt. He rang me.

Francis   Goo did?

Chick   No, Goo didn't ring me. What the fuck would Goo be ringing me for? Mousey rang me. How are you, he says. Brian Gannon here, you'll remember me from school.
Didn't mean a thing.

Francis   Mousey?

Chick   Mousey. Side parting, kind of furry.
He's in PR now. Got his own company.

Francis   Mousey?

Chick Mousey! His mother was in the choir. Big breasts like the Sierra Nevada.

Francis Mousey Gannon! Brian Gannon.

Chick Exactly!

Beat.

Francis What about him?

Chick He's got a client. His client has a big job for the right agency. Mousey is very excited.

Francis Who's the client?

Chick You won't believe this.

Francis What?

Chick Are you ready for this?

Francis What?

Chick You're not going to fucking believe this.

Francis What?

Chick The Christian Brothers.

Francis Fuck off?

Chick They want a recruitment campaign.

Francis Fuck off?

Chick Yep.

Francis Why you? Why did he come to you?

Chick The client wants something restrained, old-fashioned. I sprang to mind. Apparently.

Francis Man, that's a lovely little job.

Chick I'm thinking this is my golden opportunity to show those pre-pubescent wankers who are trying to fire me a thing or two about advertising. I'm thinking bijou office on

the square with a permanent parking place and saying
farewell to my haemorrhoids.

Java *arrives with a glass. She has caught the end of* **Chick***'s speech.
She smiles at him sympathetically.*

Java It's an age thing. Have you tried tea-tree oil?

Francis Java, have a seat, rest your . . . rest your /

Chick Are you on?

Francis What?

Chick Write the campaign. Retire.

Francis I've already retired. I'm a writer.

Chick My hole you retired. You just took your eye off the
ball.

Francis I chose to leave.
(*To* **Java**.) I chose to leave. Creative differences.

Chick Seven, they want seven words. The client is very
specific. I say, Mousey, seven is my lucky number. He says,
it's fuck all to do with luck. He says, are you up to it? I say,
absolutely. I told him you'd write it.

Francis *laughs.*

Chick He remembered you from school. Always pulling
the rich girlies with your Pink Floyd LPs. You had his
respect.

Francis Seven words?

Chick Seven words. Java, tell him. It won't kill him.

Java He's a writer, right? You can write seven words.

Francis Recruitment campaign for the Christian
Brothers?

Chick Seven words. Join the lads for . . .

Francis Travel, security, under-age sex.

Chick   That's four words.

Francis   That's five.

Chick   That's fine. I am old. I am already old. I turned to look at the view and when I turned back I was . . .
Do you realise how old we are?

Francis (*to* **Java**)   So what else do you do when you're not being a mermaid?

Java   I'm a student.

Francis   What do you study?

Java   Psychology and herbalism.

Francis   Fantastic. Psychology and herbalism.

Java   And event management on Wednesdays.

Chick   I'm driving back from the airport. I'm feeling good, pulling the magnets off the dash. I have Mousey reverberating through the speakers like an ambitious DJ. I tell him we're considering his offer.

Francis   You what?

Chick   Mousey is laughing like he needs a piss, the way he used to in the showers. He's saying there's money to be made here. These guys need to be dragged from the brink of extinction, they'd sell their mothers for a few recruits. I'm playing hardball. I say: 'Jesus, Mousey, you can't give it away. Nobody is interested in public service any more. Who wants to be a civil servant, a soldier, a priest? It is not a very fucking sexy career choice.' 'But,' says Mousey, 'where would *you* be today without the sacrifice, the dedication of the priest?'

Francis (*to* **Java**)   This is all before your time.

Chick   'It may be sexy to be secular,' he says – he always was a smart bollix – 'but without the educator, without the feckin leather, you'd still be shuffling in the bog, sticking your wango in a sheep.'

Java   God!

Chick   Sorry.

Francis (*to* **Java**)   Herbalism?

Chick   It's a lovely airport.

Francis   What?

Chick (*to* **Java**)   It's a lovely airport. Have you seen it?

Java   Yeah.

Francis   Of course she's seen the airport. She's practically a fucking doctor.

Chick   It's a beautiful airport. It is a monument to our prosperity. Depart, arrive, eat, drink, perfumes, smoked fish, billboards, big fucking billboards, join the winning team, we apologise for inconvenience during renovation. We should have known. All those years of humiliation and badly fitting confirmation suits were leading to this . . . this glorious tribute to our modernity. Mousey is right. We have fucking arrived and it's thanks to the men in black. They could have made pilots of all of us.

Pause. **Chick**, *waiting for a response from* **Francis**, *begins to scratch.*

Francis   You look awful.

Chick   I'm sick. I don't sleep.

Java   Have you tried acupuncture?

Francis (*to* **Java**)   You're a doctor, tell him he looks awful.

Java   Herbs. Try herbs and an Indian head massage.

Francis   Take a pill, have a check-up.

Chick (*to* **Java**)   I am on my fucking knees, literally. As soon as Mr Creative here left, they put my desk under the stairs. I have a permanent scar from attempting to stand.

He shows her.

Java   Arnica.

Chick   He was the best. The industry is a lesser place without him.

Francis   'Control . . . at the tip of your fingers.' Java, say 'Naturally'.

Java   Naturally.

Francis   Say it soft.

Java   Naturally.

Francis   Say it again.

Java   Naturally.

Francis   You're in the wrong job.
(*To* **Chick**.) Write it down.

Beat.

Seven words. We need research. What would make some young guy join the Brothers? In this day and age, what? What is a vocation? Java . . .

Java (*alarmed*)   What?

Francis   Seven words to make you join the Christian Brothers?

Java   Free clothes.

Francis   That's two.

Java   Holidays.

Francis   Three.

Java   World peace.

Francis   An altruistic five.

Java   My boyfriend was already a member.

Francis   Your boyfriend?

Java   Maybe not.

Chick I better go.

Java Don't.

Chick I've got to get back to the office, some copy to write. Control at the tip of your / love it.
(*To* **Francis**.) We're on?

Francis Set something up with Mousey, something informal.

Chick Sure.

Francis And, eh, hope Dessie's / OK.

Chick Thanks.

Java Who's Dessie?

Chick My brother. He used to be a priest, now he's a . . .

Francis Now he's a demonstration bunny.

Java Bunny rabbit?

Chick Bunny rabbit, yes.

Java That's a big change for him.

Beat.

Chick Yes.

Beat.

Cheers.

Francis Call me.

Exit **Chick**.

Psychologist? Better watch myself. You might read my mind.

Java Psychology student.

Beat.

And you're a writer?

Francis   Yes.

Java   What do you write?

Francis   Fiction.

Java   You're a fictional writer.

Francis   I'm a writer of fiction.

Java   That's what I meant.

Pause.

Francis   What moves you, Java? What bores you? I'm interested in you. As a writer.

Java   Yeah? Em. I dunno really. Loads of stuff moves me, or outrages me. War. I feel . . .

Francis   Yeah?

Java   Powerless. Mainly.

Beat.

Moon landings, I get bored shitless by moon landings.
I dunno. I dunno how to answer your question. It's too big.

Francis   Let me film you.

Java   What?

Francis   Research, for my book. I ask you a couple of questions, video your response.

Java   What's it like, being a writer?

Francis   Liberating. Lonely.

Java   I've never met a real writer before.

Francis   Really.

Java   Loads of guys, like, think they're writers you know, or think if you think they're a writer they're going to get laid.

Francis   Cheap.

Java   Yeah.

Francis   Writing is a remarkably physical profession. You need the stamina of an athlete.

Java   Really?

Francis   The work, functions on many levels.

Java   Right /

Francis   Many levels of consciousness.

Java   OK.

Francis   My current novel /

Java   Uh-huh.

Francis   A very filmic novel.

Java   Yeah?

Francis   It's about a very beautiful young woman shackled to an overbearing patriarch. That's on one level. Now, for young woman, read society; for patriarch, read church. A church that demands passivity, and a beautiful young woman who yearns for experience.

Java   What happens?

Francis   Well, the patriarch . . .

Java   Church /

Francis   . . . driven by his own carnality, attacks her. The very society he feeds off.

Java   What does she do?

Francis   She meets an outsider, a knowledgeable, sophisticated man, a man whose touch opens her like a box .

Java   And for outsider, read?

Francis   Art. Culture.

Beat.

Java   What's her name, the beautiful young woman?

Francis   I haven't decided yet.

Java   Call her . . .

Francis   What?

Java   Call her Java.

Francis   That's your name.

Java   I know.

They kiss.

Scene Three

Beach. Sounds of hospital paging system and canteen.

Magda *is sitting on a hospital canteen chair.*

Magda   My father took a lover. She was tall. She'd had her teeth straightened. She said of my father: 'He has beautiful feet, he has the feet of Jesus.' Unfortunately she said it to my mother, who suspected the worst.

My father's lover had a husband. Gin and lime drinker, voice like a mastiff. He had one joke, which he told, often: 'What lies shivering on the bottom of the ocean? A nervous wreck. Do you get it? a nervous wreck.'

Beat.

We laughed.
He was a rich man, influential.

My father's lover lived, childlessly, in a low white house on the road to the shore. She slept late. When she woke up she drove to Ozzie's seafront hotel with the heated swimming pool, where she swam up and down keeping her face out of the chlorine while a big grey sea howled outside the glass.

We called it Ozzie's. Because it was Ozzie's hotel. It had a name, the Bay View, but that's the thing about living on a peninsula, you like to personalise everything, you like to distinguish yourself from the trainloads of dowdy families that litter your streets. You are *us* and everyone else is *them*, so we, the locals, *us*, we went to Ozzie's and lolled around in his Swedish sauna not looking at each other's genitals for fear of being thought parochial.

On Saturdays he brought me to her home to visit. She had a cat who ignored me. 'Play with the cat,' he said. Then they'd disappear and we would glare at each other, the cat and I, while *my* father fucked *its* meal ticket in the guest bedroom.

In the car, he'd say: 'Who did we not see today?'

We'd go home then. He'd have a sandwich, take a nap, before heading down to Ozzie's.

I was seven. I was happy. I liked routine.

Sound effects of hospital.

Alone with my mother in our windy house with the sand blasting our back door, I would draw a moustache over my upper lip with a piece of my father's charcoal. 'What,' I'd ask her, 'lies shivering at the bottom of the ocean? A nervous wreck. Do you get it? Do you?' And we'd laugh, my mother and I, we'd laugh.

Sound effects of hospital.

When it got late, we would get under the big blanket and, in the warmth – the tip of her cigarette like a busy little alien, her breath like paraffin.

We chatted about overdosing, watching Doris Day and Rock Hudson climbing into twin beds with all their make-up on. 'See their bedside lockers?' she'd say. 'Crammed with pills. Their lockers are crammed with pills. *That* is the way to go: silk pyjamas, a locker full of Valium, and Rock Hudson three feet of tufty carpet away.' When she was drunk she talked like an American. Let's put some gas in the car, she used to say. She called it that – gas.

One day Ozzie was on the telephone. 'You must come down, Kit, we never see you any more.'

That, I wanted to say to him, was because we were busy watching Doris and Rock movies and storing up the aspirin, and because there was a sapling growing out of our living-room floor. There was a tree growing in our living room, a black-leaf chestnut had burst through the floor. Spring had been tricky. The foliage was obliterating the telly. My mother thought the little tree was courageous.

We tied the sapling to the table leg. My mother apologised to it.

It was near her birthday when Ozzie rang. The sapling was restless, wouldn't oblige, wouldn't bend. The sapling was getting stronger; every time we tried to tie it to the table leg it snapped back. We could *hear* Brucie – cuddly toy, Teasmade, toaster, fondue set, hostess trolley – but we couldn't see him, just a lot of greenery. Blackery.

'We'll go,' she said. 'We'll take Ozzie up on his invitation. We'll go to Ozzie's seafront hotel.'

Sound effects of hospital.

Scene Four

Bathroom.

Chick, *in underwear, shirt, socks, sits on the edge of the toilet attempting to make a telephone call on* **Louise**'s *highly decorative phone.*

Chick   Hello, could you tell me . . . ? Sorry, sure.

Pause.

Hello, cou . . . Hello, Paul. I'm looking for the code for . . .
Sure, sorry . . .

Louise, *robed, steps out of the shower. She unwraps and shakes her hair.*

Chick   Louise!

Louise   What?

Chick   Hair.

Louise   Sorry /

Chick   Hello? Oh hello, Paul, yes, I was looking for the code for /

Louise   Who's Paul?

Chick   What?
(*To phone.*) Sorry /

Louise   Paul? Who's Paul?

Chick   The operator.
(*To phone.*) Sorry?
(*To* **Louise**.) Sorry, the customer service representative.

Louise   Oh.

Louise *begins conditioning her hair.*

(*To phone.*) Yes, Webster City in Iowa. Iowa /

Louise   Dessie?

Chick   Yeah.
(*To phone.*) Sorry?

Louise   Alex said I had clammy hands. Are my hands clammy? I do not have clammy hands.

Chick   What? International /

Louise   It's adolescent.

Chick   She *is* adolescent.
(*To phone.*) International, sure . . .

Louise   She's eleven, for Christ's sake.

Chick   Louise, please.
(*To phone.*) Sorry. Hello, Paul / gone.

He redials.

Louise   I think, OK, it's a phase /

Chick   Damn.

He redials.

Louise   I'll be friendly. I'll pick her up from school /

Chick   Sorry. Paul. You're not Paul . . .

He has been cut off, redials.

Louise   Suggest a late lunch.

Chick   At four?

Louise   It's not without precedent /

Chick   No.

Louise   To have lunch at four.

Chick   No.

Louise   It's flexible.

Chick   Right.

Louise   It should be a flexible meal, right?

I am at the school gates. Ten to four. I am checking my shoulders for dandruff when Shanaz arrives.

Arrives? She nearly runs over me. The bloody car could flatten villages. Takes all six stone of her to turn the wheel. She pulls up, she pulls in, she parks. *Ça va /*

Chick   Is there something on the back of my neck?

Louise   No.

Chick (*to phone*)   Hello /

Louise   'La bus', Shanaz calls it. Tiers of seats.

Chick (*to* **Louise**)   They're busy.

Louise   Girls stream out of school.

Chick   Neck, Louise.

Louise   Two of them are Shanaz's. Alex is with them.

Chick   Back of my neck /
(*To phone.*) Hello?

Louise   Alex sees me and looks devastated.
There is nothing on your neck. 'How was Normandy?' I ask
Shanaz, without much conviction because I can't remember
where she told me she was buying. France, of course I
should have just said, 'How was France?' Cover my arse.

Chick   Your derrière.
(*Shouting.*) Hello?

Louise   'God, no,' she says. 'Not Normandy, it was never
Normandy, no. Souillac, Dordogne.

Chick   Hello!

Louise   'Three hectares with a possible further fifteen, bay
windows, a barn and a bread oven.'

Chick   It's itchy. My neck is itchy.

Louise   'Sounds fantastic,' I say. Alex is glaring at me.
Sukie and Tashi are hoisting themselves into 'La Bus'.
'Spring water,' says Shanaz, 'straight from the well. Not
cheap as French properties go, but hey . . .' Stop scratching.

She smacks **Chick***'s hand away.*

'Hell,' I say. I'm making a joke now. 'You could always
bottle the water.' 'No,' she says. 'No, no, it's just for our own
consumption.' And she looks at me, and now I'm crass *and*
fat.

Chick You are not /
(*To phone.*) Oh, hello? Hello, yes, hello, Ed. I'm trying to
telephone Webster City . . .

Louise Stop scratching! You'll make it worse.

Chick (*to* **Louise**) What worse? (*To phone.*) Webster,
Webster City?

Louise I can tell Alex wants to get in with them.

Chick Hello?
(*To* **Louise**.) He's gone. Ed's gone.

Louise I say: 'Hey, Alex, how about a late lunch?'
'Oh God,' she says, 'not more food.'

Chick 'It'. You said 'it', you'll make *it* worse.
(*To phone.*) Hello? Ed?

Louise Alex is hissing at me that she's arranged to go
home with Sukie and Tashi. 'Come on, Lexi,' says Shanaz,
like she's calling the Labrador. And Lexi scales 'La Bus' and
sits next to Sukie and Tashi, who are flicking their 'I'm
worth it too' ponytails at me – and the windows hiss closed.
And away they go, Lexi's triumphant little face and
Shanaz's bloody continental fingers, which are waving and
which I want to break.

Chick (*to phone*) Hello, hello. Ed. Come back, Ed.

Louise I am now standing alone outside the school gates.
So I go to the supermarket to get her something organic for
her tea and make the fatal bloody error of putting a packet
of hydrogenised animal fat muffins in the creaking trolley.
And then I see it, the test.

Chick (*to* **Louise**) What test?
(*To phone.*) Hello?

Louise I'm retaining a lot of fluid, my ankles are like
lifebelts.

Chick What test?

Louise   I'm wearing my rings on a chain around my neck.

Chick   What test?
(*To phone.*) Yes! Zero zero /

Louise   I already had my suspicions.

Chick   Suspiscions? What suspicions?
(*To phone.*) Zero zero one five one five . . . Thank you!

Louise   I throw it in the trolley. I turn.

Chick   Pen! Louise!

Louise   Anne-Marie 'keep it simple to be in touch with nature' is pushing down the aisle. She has nothing. I swear the woman has nothing in her trolley but balsamic vinegar and rice cakes.

Chick   Pen!

He begins dialling a long complicated number from a notebook he takes from his shirt pocket and balances on his knee.

Louise   She has a child in Alex's class, it goes everywhere hooded.

Chick (*in a whisper*)   Eight. Seven. Seven. Seven. Nine. Two. Three.

Louise   She has no thighs, her face is bagging over her jaw like a collapsed balloon. She was a normal girl once. She tells me she's doing a fun run for the homeless.

Chick (*starting again*)   Louise!

Louise   'That's not for you, Louise?' she says.

Chick   Louise!

Louise   She sounds . . . reproach /

Chick   Louise!

Louise   It is a reproachful sound. She is talking to me, pointing at the predictor test, which her normally docile eyes have detected under the pile of shampoos and

conditioners and rinses and de-tanglers and anti-frizzes that
I have been dropping, discreetly I thought, on top of the
pack in the vainglorious hope that the sagging bag won't
notice it. 'That can't be for you, love.'

Chick (*shouting*)   Louise. Stop.

Louise   Can you believe it? You'd get more juice out of a
prune, and she's calling me 'love'.
'God no,' I said. 'What would I want with that?'

Chick   It's ringing . . .
(*To phone.*) Wal-Mart, central Webster City, Iowa?

Louise   I said I'd sponsor her, put money on her to run
her jangly arse around the park for an hour so she could
step over people in doorways with impunity.

Chick (*to phone*)   I'm trying to locate an employee, my
brother . . . No . . . How many?

Louise   Of course, it's like bloody proms night when the
mobile phone rings. You'd think the London Symphony
Orchestra was in the damn supermarket, because Lexi,
formerly known as Alex, has changed the sodding ring.

Chick (*to phone*)   He's a recent /

Louise   I say: 'Is that you who changed the ring?'
She's talking very quietly. I assume Tashi and Tikiboo are
in earshot.
She says: 'Your ring embarrassed me.'
'Excuse the fuck out of me,' I say.

Chick   Promotions /

Louise   I liked the theme tune from *The Virginian*. It
reminded me of my mother.

Chick (*to phone.*)   Hello?
(*To* **Louise**) You're depressed. You are depressed, Louise.
Take a Xanax. Get control, Louise, keep *a grip*.

Louise   She wants me to pick her up. Sukie and Malooki are going for a hot tub at the Murphys'. Alex doesn't want to go, she's developing a bikini line.

Chick (*very frustrated, to phone*)   Hello?

Louise   I did not think it humanly possible to develop a bikini line at eleven; she, however, informs me that it is and she is. The shock of being the recipient of such privileged information makes me temporarily forget that I dislike her and I throw an exfoliant into the trolley. When I looked up, Anne-Marie was gone.

Chick (*to phone*)   Please . . .

Louise   I peed on the stick. The blue line is what you're waiting for. Well, I'm just sitting there on the downstairs WC looking at these little windows of opportunity and they're looking back at me.

Chick   Louise /

Louise   The blue line /

Chick (*to phone*)   Yes, I'll hold.

Louise   The blue line /

Chick   Louise, take a fucking pill.

Louise   Listen to me.

Chick   I do not need this from you right now, Louise, I do not need this.

Louise   You have no idea of the fight I make to surface for you /

Chick   Where are your pills?

Louise   To have a coherent thought under the weight of this . . .

Chick   Where are your pills, Louise?

Louise   I ground them up and gave them to the dog.

Chick (*angry, to phone*)   I *am* holding.

Louise   I'm sitting at the kitchen table. I have made a wall of hair products, I have spread jam on the muffins . . .

Chick (*angry, to phone*)   I don't know. He's a bunny rabbit. How many fucking bunny rabbits have you got in Webster City?

Louise   My mouth is a trapdoor to my past. I can see my mother . . . /

Chick (*shouting*)   Louise, shut up /

Louise   My mother marching up and down the seafront in big plastic paddy pants, plastic bags wrapped around her waist and thighs to burn off the fat . . . /

Chick   Fuck it /

He hangs up.

Louise   . . . and the banana and milk diet, and the boiled chicken diet, and the Limmits biscuits and the PLJ. That woman could count calories in her sleep, and where did that get her? Where? Tell me?

Chick   Stop.

Louise   I hear my name being called. I look up.
And there is Shanaz in her raw-silk pedal-pushers and her kilim slippers and her skinny-knit vest-top with a look of concern on her nut-brown face that would earn her a job on television.

Beat. **Chick** *stares at her.*

'Louise, love, are you all right?' Love, I am so grateful to hear it. / 'You are fat,' Alex says. / Shanaz rattling her keys, not making any unnecessary facial movements for fear of being permanently burdened with expression. / I say: 'We didn't have it easy, did we?'

Chick (*quietly*)   Stop stop stop talking. Stop talking.

Louise   I hear 'La Bus' go. I hear Lexi running after it, and I finished the fucking animal fat muffins, all twelve of them.

Pause.

Chick (*defeated*)   You told me you were on top of things. We were going to have a normal life, the three of us, a normal bloody life.

Louise   Normal life? Saturday nights watching you get rat-arsed over your Chinese takeaway and your nostalgia TV? Watching some has-been DJ make you weep with a selection of hits from 1979?

Chick   What's wrong with 1979? I was happy in 1979.

Louise   Of course you were happy in 1979. You were young, you were thin. We were all happy in 1979.

Chick   You are depressed, that's all, you're just depressed.

Louise   I'm pregnant.

Pause.

Chick   You let me /

Louise   I wanted this /

Chick   You let me fuck you knowing /

Louise   Yes, I did, and you fucked me like I was marbling on a slab.

Phone rings very loudly to the tune of 'Frère Jacques'.

I want this baby.

Chick *picks up phone.*

Louise   I'm ordering a birthing pool.

Chick   Des?

Chick   Des. Jesus, Dessie.
(*To* **Louise**.) It's Dessie.

Scene Five

Beach.

Francis *sits on the side of his messed-up bed, dressing.* **Java**, *half dressed, reads his manuscript, glancing up at the video, which plays another interview in the background.*

> **Elderly Man** I think about her every day. I talk to her. I know she will be there when it is my time. I pray. I pray every day to be reunited with her. With all that I have lost. She comes to me in dreams, she waits for me. I dreamt last night that I was in a crowded waiting room. My name was being called. I looked up and there she was. I never knew such sadness on waking. To lose her again. I lose her again and again. What was the question? I've forgotten the . . .

Francis Java, get dressed.

Java I want a bath.

Francis I'll drive you home. It's late.

Java So?

Java *puts down novel and rewinds the video.*

Francis I wish you'd be more careful. My equipment is very sensitive.

Java Ditto.

Pause.

Francis Java, get dressed.

Java No.

Francis Come on, I'll take you home.

Java I don't want to go home. Your book /

Francis Treatment. Yes? What about my treatment?

Java I don't like it.

She begins to rewind video further. Snippet of Taxi Driver speech, then silence.

Francis   I see. Talk about it in the car, shall we?

Java   I liked some bits of it.

Francis   Which bits?

*An image has caught **Java**'s attention. She turns up volume with remote control.*

Java   I liked the bit in the confessional.

Francis   Did you?

Video, very loud: old man's voice singing 'Mac the Knife'.

Java, turn that off, come on.

Java   Who is that?

Francis (*beginning to stand*)   Turn him off.

Video.

    Jakey   Sit down, you fool.

Francis *sits.*

Java   Wow!

    Jakey   Cyclops.

    Francis   It's a camera, Jakey. I'd like to ask you a couple of questions.

    Jakey   Stop squinting.

Francis   Turn him off, Java.

    Francis   I'm not squinting, Jakey. I'd like to interview you.

    Jakey   Do you dream? Do your dreams have a little scroll of digits in the corner?

    Francis   Jakey, this camera is a technological aid to memory. It's compact, portable /

Jakey   Give me some money, I want to get drunk.

Francis   Jake, I'd like to talk to you. Research. For my book.

Jakey   Ha!

Francis (*to* **Java**)   Turn him off.

Francis   I'd like to talk about God and sex.

Jakey   You want guidance? Information?

Francis   Opinion.

Jakey   There are two guiding principles in life.

Francis   Right. Which are?

Jakey   Inebriation and ejaculation. Now fuck off and let me get on with my work.

Francis *turns off video.*

Java   Who is he?

Francis   Get dressed.

Java   Who is he?

Francis   He's my father-in-law. Here.

He starts firing clothes at her.

Java   What is he?

Francis   He's a painter. Jakey. Forget it. Different era.

Java   What does he paint?

Francis   Women.

Java   Film me.

Francis   What?

Java   You said you were going to film me.

She walks to the top of the bed and sits. Wearing a sheet, she arranges herself to be interviewed. She is very still, becomes a painting.

Francis   You need to leave.

Java   Film me. You said you were going to film me. That's what we came here for, remember?

Francis   Tomorrow.

Java   I think you brought me here under false pretences. Film me!

Francis   No.

She becomes entirely still.

Java!

Java   I can't hear you. I'm made of stone.

Francis *hurriedly takes up camera.*

Francis   Fuck, Java, this is not funny. What time is it? Research. Subject: girl. God and sex. Go. Talk.

Java   Talk about what? You haven't asked me a question yet.

Francis   Do you believe in God?

Java   No. I'm a humanist.

Francis   Fascinating. Thank you.

He begins to switch off camera.

Java   You know what's the problem with your story?

Francis (*still filming*)   No.

Java   You got God wrong.

Francis   Really?

Java   And you got sex wrong.

Francis   The genesis of the story is the struggle between faith and desire.

Java   Yeah?

Francis   Yeah.

Java   You've made sex like a big gymkhana.

Francis   Well, thank you for the unsolicited literary criticism /

Java   When do they get to chill? Your God is for boys.

Francis   What?

Java   Your God is for boys and your sex is all sport.

Pause.

Francis   Get dressed.

Java   I feel like talking.

Francis   Not now.

He turns off camera.

Java   Do you still like me?

Francis   Less.

Java   Humanists believe life can be lived to the full while respecting the opinions of others.

Francis   Given that you are straddling my wife's bed, Java, I would have to say yours is a very fragile dogma. Get dressed.

Java   It is not a dogma or a religion. Kiss me.

Francis   Why are you doing this?

Java   I like you.

Francis   Go home.

Java   My boyfriend's not expecting me back yet.

Francis   Your boyfriend a humanist too?

Java   He's a pantheist. He's coming back as a tree.

She walks down the bed, takes the camera from **Francis**. *She starts kissing him.*

Do you sleep here with your wife?

Francis   You really need to go now.

Java   Will you dedicate your book to me?

Francis   What book?

Java   I think it would make a great movie.

Francis   Yeah?

Java   Do you love your wife?

Beat.

Francis   Of course.

Java   Is your wife beautiful?

Francis   Not as beautiful as you.

Java *continues kissing him.*

You should go.

Java   Why does the old man treat you like a fool?

Francis   It's a ritual. He thinks I'm shallow.

Java   You *are* shallow. Shallow is fine. Shallow's a beach. What do you want to be, Van Gogh? Homer? Those guys are all dead with missing body parts.

Francis   Homer didn't have any missing body parts.

Java   That you know?

Beat.

Can I meet him? Will he paint me?

Francis   He's dying.

Pause. **Francis** *gets upset.*

Java   Do you love him?

Francis   He's a cruel fucker. Makes me feel like a piece of shit. You just want him to acknowledge you, fucking buy you a drink, anything. He mops people up. He remains unscathed.

Pause.

You are beautiful. You are so fucking beautiful.

Java   I won't always be.

Francis   No. You will grow old.

He kisses her.

Go home.

Java   No.

*As **Java** drops sheet, lights go down.*

Scene Six

Beach, empty except for swivel chair and sheets of paper blowing across the stage. Sound effects of office equipment and distant conspiratorial voices.

Chick   I am depressed. It's nothing I can't handle. It manifests . . . It is physical. It is a physical depression.

I shit in white. Little white pellets. I shit like a Chihuahua. I itch. I have patches, eczematic patches on my legs, my feet, my ankles. Apnoea? I have it. I don't sleep at night, I die. My chest is bruised from my wife thumping it to restart my heart.

My heart. I have neglected my heart.

I have knotted veins in my arse, panic attacks, hot flushes, cold sweats. I ejaculate in my sleep like a fucking altar boy. I am lost. My gums bleed.

I was a happy child. They say that matters, they say that counts for something.

There were two of us. Me and my brother. Me and Dessie. Our father was a magician. Our mother assisted him. They did kids' parties. They weren't particularly successful, although I don't know how you measure success in that profession. Lack of scarring, maybe.

Our father was diabetic. He wore a hairpiece.

Dessie was older than me, years older. Mostly he sat under the kitchen table ignoring me, reading paperback books about girls in boarding school. I didn't know him very well. He was a seminarian by the time I was nine. I think my mother got to him – the holy pictures glued on to her make-up box, the scapular of Oliver Plunkett sewn into her bra top that glittered and smelt of cats. The rattle of her doves in the box. I think he went to the seminary to finish his book, get a bit of peace. Or maybe he knew more than me. People do.

Sometimes I think I miss all the important bits. I miss the central bit that makes other things make sense.

One day, when I was looking at myself in the bathroom mirror, she left. She got into a blue car parked at the end of our road, or so the butcher said. He was a good butcher, a very good butcher, a family butcher, but we never held that against him. She left the doves, God bless her.

Dessie took over making the tea for us. Until he went into the seminary. He'd heard his name being called, he said, clear as a bell. So we waited a bit longer for my mother and when the summer season came around again and she still hadn't turned up we took the train to Butlins without her, my father and I, to audition for the summer season. We had her birds in the box. We looked out the windows. Kept ourselves to ourselves. We were the professionals. My mother had told me that animals went to heaven and God was a smoker. I decided on that train that my mother had died, in some glorious blameless way. I sat by that window, saw her in the clouds, chatting with God over a cup of tea and a fag, whooshing the cat off the ledge.

We arrived at Butlins. I thought I was in Hollywood. It was 1968.

We waited in the restaurant for our audition. You could look up from there into the glass-bottomed swimming pool at a ceiling of independent legs and torsos splashing about.

I thought, a really good magician would reattach those limbs to their owners. A really good magician would bring back the dead.

Scene Seven

Beach. Bedroom set-up as in Scene Five. Dawn. Flickering light from the video.

Magda *is reading typescript.*

Francis *comes in quietly.*

Francis   I thought you'd be asleep.

Magda   I was. I had a dream.

Francis   It's late / you . . .

Magda   I dreamt I was at a border crossing. It was hot. There was an official. He gave me a bag of shit, told me I'd have to eat it before I could cross to the other side. I started eating it. I woke up.

Pause. **Magda** *continues watching video.*

Francis   How's Jakey? Any change?

Magda   His fingers are black. He's cold.

Francis   That's not actually ready / for

Magda   You have a scratch, on your face.

Francis   Do I? I've been swimming.

Magda   In what/ Cutlery?

Francis   Shaving, I meant to say shaving.

Magda *stares at him.*

Francis   That's not actually ready / for

Magda *flicks through pages.*

Francis   It's not ready / for you

Magda (*reading*)   'Wearily he leaned his long frame against the studio door, the intoxicating aroma of oils and linseed a soothing olfactory balm against the rancid street below.'

Beat.

Not that bit?

Francis   It's not . . . ready.

Magda   No.
'Gradually the bustling / intrusion . . . '

Francis   It's not ready.

Magda   'Gradually the bustling intrusion of the outside world ebbed away and, hungrily gnawing on his meagre husk of loaf, he once again returned to his art.'

She laughs.

Francis   What? What's funny?

Magda   'Meagre husk of loaf.'

Francis   Yeah?

Magda   It's funny. It's really very funny.

Francis   Magda!

He tries to take the typescript. Flicking through pages, **Magda** *continues to read.*

Magda   'Hold me, she beseeched, I am beyond redemption now, surely God would spurn me, knowing the baseness of my thoughts, the depth of my desire for you. Wearily . . .' There's old 'wearily' again . . .

Francis   Magda!

Magda   'Wearily he tried to resist her, her flesh like a new young plum pulsating in his hand. He reached for her mouth, tasted her youth, rolled it around his mouth like a promise.'

She stops, closes the typescript.

You know the really sad thing, Francis?

Francis   No.

Magda   Someone is bound to publish you.

Beat.

Francis   Give me my manuscript.

Magda (*shouting*)   Take it, fucking take it. This time I will leave you.

Francis   What are you talking about

Magda   Where did you take her, home? You've been a long time.

Francis   Sorry.

Magda   She's beautiful. But so young. God.

Francis   What / are you . . .

Magda   I watched you.

Francis   You / what?

Magda   I watched you leave with her. I was about to get out of my car. They started playing Louis Armstrong on the radio, the one Jakey sings.

Francis   Mac / the . . .

Magda (*shouting*)   It doesn't fucking matter what it's called.

Francis   I was working. She's a student . . . Research . . . I . . . Zeitgeist . . . She's helping me with the book. Christ.

Magda   Get out.

Francis   We're not all like your father, fucking anything with a pulse /

Magda   I said get out.

Pause.

You brought her to my bed.

Pause.

Francis (*quietly*)   She understands me.

Magda   Sorry?

Francis   She understands me, understands my work.

Magda   Your work.

Francis   My book.

Magda   This is not a *book*, this is a little bit of wistful pornography.

Francis   Supply and demand Magda. Supply and demand. It's the fucking market place Magda. People want a book to slap them round a bit, relieve the tedium of a fat wife or a slow bus. It's a fucking transaction Magda. It's not art Magda. Is that what you want me to say? Well says who? Says fucking who it's not art?

Magda   It's shit.

Francis   Your *problem*, Magda, is that you speak a dead language. It is no surprise to me that you don't understand my work.

Magda   I understood your work perfectly. Your work is bullshit. In any language.

Francis   What you read . . . what you read is a metaphor.

Magda   It's not a metaphor. It's bullshit.

Francis   It's contemporary, it's populist. So fucking what?

Magda   It's not contemporary /

Francis   Even your father knew how to sell to the man on the street. Everybody loves a pair of tits /

Magda   His work is figurative.

Francis   Perfectly acceptable to have a pair of tits hanging over the mantelpiece once they've got Jakey's signature on them.

Magda   His work is figurative, not pornographic.

Francis   Tell that to your mother. The galleries have made picture postcards of her cunt /

Magda   Don't. Don't say it.

Francis   I've had it. (*He stands to leave.*) Sorry, Magda, I'm sick of being held up to Jakey for some measure of my work, of my credibility.

Magda   Where are you going?

Francis   Why me, Magda? Why did you choose me?

Pause.

Magda   Because you weren't him. You, your work, your campaigns seemed so uncomplicated. Comforting. It felt like normal life.

Francis   A normal life? Is that what you were after, Magda? All these years? A normal life?

Magda   Where are you going?

Francis   You can't make me a happy lay-the-decking chappie on the edge of this little bay. I have a bigger agenda, Magda. I happen to have a bigger life to lead.

Francis *starts to leave.*

Magda   I don't know what I am supposed to do. When my mother was my age, she was dead. If she was alive I'd have someone to talk to, I'd have somewhere to go.

Francis   She was a lush. If she was alive you'd hate her.

Magda *breaks down.*

Magda   Tonight. Tonight I stood outside his room with my fingers in my ears while the nurses turned him and he howled. He howled with rage that it has come to this. That *he* has come to this. To women in surgical gloves turning him and turning him and turning him.

Francis   Magda, stop.

Magda   He won't die. He won't accept defeat. And I have to feel *sorry*. I have to touch him. Hold his hand and feel sorry. Because it's over and it has come to this, to dying. To being alone. He is dying.

Francis   I love you Magda, I always will.

Magda   You bring that child to my bed. You bring her to my bed. They turn him and turn him and you bring her to our bed.

She is diestressed. **Francis** *waits. Eventually* **Magda** *sits up and looks at him standing ready to leave.*

Francis   I want to go, Magda. I want to know who I am without you I want to go.

Pause.

Magda   This bigger life you have to lead, Francis, in shopping malls and cardboard television studios, signing your books and talking about your writing – I think you're going to be very good at it.

Francis   Jakey and I are really not that different.

Magda   Jakey had one redeeming quality: talent.

Beat.

Unfortunately, Francis, fucking other people's daughters and growing a goatee doesn't compensate for lack of it.

Pause. Then **Francis** *storms out. Beat. He returns picks up his mobile telephone that he has put down at the beginning of the scene. As he turns to leave again* **Magda** *hurls typescript at him.*

Interval.

Act Two

Scene One

The beach is lit for night, with fairy lights. There is an assortment of deckchairs.

Chick *is trying to get a barbecue going.* **Mousey** *sits expansively in the loudest, biggest deckchair. There is a light rain, which he and* **Chick** *notice as they talk, brushing drops off their clothes, glancing anxiously at the sky.*

Mousey You've done well for yourself, Chick. Who'd have thought it, eh?

Chick Stop.

Mousey Hiding your light under a bushel, were you, all those years?

Chick Ah now.

Mousey The Brothers beat the shite out of you for being stupid. Must have done you some good, hah?

Chick Ah sure.

Mousey How's Dessie? How's the brains of the family?

Chick What's that?

Mousey Dessie? How's Dessie?

Chick Dessie, he, eh . . .

Mousey No flies on our Dessie. Christian Brother, isn't he?

Chick That's right, he's . . . / em . . . .

Mousey What's that?

Chick He's great, fine.

Mousey   Good, good. Won't do you any harm with the boys having a Brother in the business, so to speak. Nice to know we're all singing off the same hymn sheet.

Chick   Yes.

Mousey   And your da is dead, God rest him. Bit of a dark horse, your da, with the abracadabraing and the paper doilies.

Chick   Origami.

Mousey   What are you saying?

Chick   Origami. It was his hobby. Paper art.

Mousey   Art. Don't fucking talk to me about art. I'm up to my bollix in it with this recruitment campaign.

Chick   Yes, exciting times. You must be . . .
(*Barbecue ignition.*) Whoops, nearly . . .

Mousey   You're not the only ad man I have on this, I have to tell you. Have another fella, bent obviously. He makes me an ad for the telly, it's in black and white – boys, boys running through fields, jumping into lakes, scaling walls. I said to him, this is not the fuckin' army you're selling. The assault course is a fuckin' metaphor, he says, for the tribulations of priesthood. Tribulations, my hole, I said to him, give me that in colour and I'll think about it. Fuckin' fags are everywhere.

Enter **Louise**.

Well, would you look at that.

Louise   Mousey. Goodness, how are you?

Mousey   Brian.

Louise   Haven't seen you / since . . .

Mousey   Brian. My name is Brian.

Louise   Sorry, I . . . Brian, of course. Lovely . . .
(*To* **Chick**.) Why don't you use the ignition thingy?

Chick   I did. Any other suggestions?

Louise   I'll get the spare.
(*Passing* **Mousey**.) Did Chick tell you I'm going to have a baby?

Exit **Louise**.

Mousey   What did she say?

Chick   She said she's going to get the gravy.

Mousey   Oh.
(*Looking after* **Louise**.) Jesus, isn't it extraordinary how women go to seed?

Chick   Sorry?

Mousey   They run to fat. Nothing they can do about it, I suppose. It's the nature of the beast. The intractable problem with women is sooner or later it's all going to collapse around their knees, and they'll be staggering around in support tights.

Chick   What?

Mousey   Fucking extraordinary how married people deteriorate. Men, married men, are single-handedly hijacking the fucking health service with obesity-related complaints.

Chick   Really?

Mousey   They're like fucking gannets, mouths hanging open for whatever mess gets put into it. Couches full of men gone to seed. Men who could be athletes, warriors. Younger men, when they're not kicking the shit out of each other, take some pride in their appearance. Do you work out, Chick? No?

Chick   No.

Mousey   Have you ever worn a body shaper, Chick?

Chick   No.

Mousey   Don't knock it till you've tried it. That thing lit yet?

Chick   No.

Mousey   No. Still, you got a couple of good years out of her. Matches, you need matches.

Beat.

So where's Francis? Where's the creative?

Chick (*looking around*)   He's, eh . . . Yes indeed . . .

Mousey   He *is* coming, right?

Chick   God, yes, yes. He wouldn't miss it for the world.

Mousey   This is big, Chick. You know what I'm saying? This is as big as it gets.

Chick   Which is . . . Which is pretty . . . big. Yes.

Mousey   Yes.

Chick   Yes.

Uncomfortable pause.

How's your wife, how's . . . ?

Mousey   Susan.

Chick   Susan. How is she?

Mousey   So-so. Not bad. Have her at the gym most days, she gets a bit sloppy if she's not pushed.

Noises, off.

Chick   Great, good, terrific, here he is. The creative has landed, as they say.

Enter **Magda** *and* **Louise**.

And Magda. Great, terrific.

Louise   Chick, Magda's here!

Chick   I see that, Louise. Fantastic. Magda.

Magda   Chick.

She goes to **Chick** *and kisses him.*

Francis here?

Chick   No. He's not with you?

Magda   No.

Chick   Oh.
(*To* **Mousey**.) Oh well, he's late. Goes with the territory.
These . . . these highly creative guys have no idea of time.
Magda, this is Mou . . . Brian. Brian Gannon.

Mousey   Magda.

Chick   Drink, Magda?

Magda   Thank you.

Mousey   Do you work out, Magda?

Magda   I beg your pardon?

Mousey   We were talking about fitness, just saying you
girls can achieve a lot with a bit of discipline.

Louise (*to* **Mousey**, *handing him the igniter*)   Maybe you'd
like to put this somewhere.

Chick   Let's make that a large one.

Magda   Thanks.

Chick (*indicating drinks*)   Louise.
(*To* **Mousey**, *about the igniter*.) I'll take that, Mousey, thanks.

Mousey   Brian.

Louise   Magenta, Magda.
(*Handing* **Mousey** *a drink*.) Here you are, Brian.

Magda   Sorry?

Mousey (*squeezing* **Louise**)   You haven't changed a bit.

Louise   You should see me in my underwear.

Mousey *looks pained.*

Louise   I'm like a blancmange.

He stops squeezing.

Chick (*to* **Mousey**)   Not a bad view, do you think?

Mousey   What's that?

Chick   View, the view – you can see the harbour.

Mousey   What's it worth, this place?

Chick   More than it used to be, I suppose.

Mousey   More than it used to be! The guy is a comedian!

Magda *is transfixed by* **Mousey**.

Louise   Magda. Magda.

Magda   Sorry. Yes.

Louise   Magenta.

Magda   Magenta. Yes?

Louise   It's a warm colour, right?

Magda   Yes . . .
(*To* **Mousey**.) Your hair is cobalt.

Louise   But is magenta a colour to produce a feeling of well-being and harmony?

Mousey   What's cobalt?

Chick   Blue.

Louise   Or is it claustrophobically womb-like?

Mousey   Blue?

Louise   Because the last thing we want . . .

Mousey (*to* **Magda**)   Blue?

Magda *nods.*

Louise   . . . is to make him feel like he's sitting in a big vagina. He's a priest, for Christ's sake.

Mousey (*to* **Chick**)   Who's sitting in a big vagina?

Chick   I have no idea.

Louise   Dessie.

Mousey   Dessie?
(*To* **Chick**.) What the fuck is Dessie doing in a big /

Louise (*to* **Magda**)   We're expecting him any day now. I'm revamping the spare room and I am absolutely torn.

Mousey (*to* **Louise**)   Dessie's coming home?

Chick   Matches, Louise.

Louise (*to* **Mousey**)   Didn't you hear? He's /

Chick   Looking forward to his visit. And he is. Matches, Louise.

Magda   No.

Chick   I need matches.

Louise   No you don't.

Chick   I do.

Mousey   He does.

Louise   You don't.

Louise *sits down.*

Chick   Fine.

Mousey   Dessie's coming home? Good.
(*To* **Magda**.) Was just telling Chick, it gives our clients a nice feeling of security, him having a brother in the business. Nice to know we're all / singing from the same hymn-sheet.

Chick   Singing from the same hymn sheet.

Magda   Terrific.

Silence.

Chick   Matches, Louise. Please, pet.

Louise   No.

Chick   Fine, I'll just light the barbecue with this banana then.

Louise   It's not a banana, it's a cleverly disguised igniter that has been designed to light the barbecue you bought against my advice, because you liked the colour.

Chick   Well, yes.

Mousey   I managed to squeeze in thirteen holes this evening.

Chick   Thirteen. Well well.

Mousey   I could eat a small child.

Chick   Matches, Louise.

Louise (*shaking her head*)   Ah-ah.

Mousey   Francis been burning the midnight oil on this campaign, Magda, has he?

Magda   I don't know. I haven't seen him. I thought he'd be here.

Chick   He's the best there is, no worries. He's a bloody good copywriter.

Magda   He's a novelist now.

Chick   Novelist, and bloody good copywriter.

Mousey (*to* **Magda**)   Novelist?

Chick (*to* **Mousey**)   Early retirement, for God's sake! Loaded, didn't need the pressure.

Magda (*to* **Mousey**)   Yes.

Louise (*to* **Mousey**)   I butterflied a lamb.

Mousey   Fantastic.

Louise   It's marinating.

Mousey   Oh.

Chick (*all the while trying and failing to light the barbecue*)   I'm not even thinking about retiring, not ready to take the scenic route just yet. I'd miss the banter, the cut and thrust, the clatter of the cappuccino machine. Shit.

Mousey   What about you, Louise? Would you not think of moving to the country? Getting a bit of exercise?

Louise   I'm *from* the country. I hated it. It's freezing.

Chick   Louise has her courses. Haven't you, pet? (*Hissing.*) Matches.

Louise   It is not designed for matches.

Mousey   So, his novel any good?

Magda   No.

Chick (*shouting at* **Louise**)   Matches!

Louise   If you want matches, you know where to find them.

Chick (*smiling*)   I can't leave go of the ignition button.

Louise   Tut.

Mousey   What's it about, this novel?

Magda   Sex and death. What's anything about?

Chick   Art. Louise.

Louise   Oh yes. My art.

Chick   She is quite a little artist, I tell you.

Magda   And faith. I think, in some obscure way, Francis is attempting to write about faith. Which should be interesting.

Chick (*to* **Mousey**)   Francis is very interested in religion. Very.

Magda   Francis isn't interested in religion, he's just enjoying the sideshow.

Chick   Another drink? Magda? Mousey? Louise, drinks, get drinks. And dips. Drinks and dips, Louise. And matches.

Magda   I think what's interesting about religion is people's persistent need for it despite all the scandal, all the sadness.

Louise   Dessie . . .

Chick   Art, Louise.

Mousey   Dessie what?

Chick   Louise!

Louise   Oh yes. I did a course in bridge painting.

Mousey   That was energetic of you. What's wrong with Dessie? I thought he was coming home for a holiday.

Chick   On canvas. We have some lovely representations of bridges.

Louise   And brooks.

Chick   And brooks.

Mousey   What wrong with Des?

Silence. **Louise** *shrugs.*

Louise   He's out in Iowa. Drink. Wham. He's got himself into a bit of a mess.

Mousey   Jesus. Nothing's been said, has it?

Louise   No. Not yet.

Mousey   Get him home. They're very litigious, Americans. Fuck-all sense of humour at the moment. Talk to me later.

Chick   I think his order are handling it.

Mousey   America is not the place to be right now. Get him home, retire him, get him a nice little job. Gardener or something. Is he any good at gardening?

Chick   I don't know. I don't really know him at all.

Louise   Last time he came home he had a perm.

Mousey   What the fuck is wrong with him?

Chick   I don't know. I don't know the man. He was lonely, I think.

Mousey   This is not good news. You realise who is employing us right now?

Chick   I know who's employing *you*, Mousey. As you said, I'm not the only candidate.

Mousey   What's that?

Magda   My memories of Iowa are a flat landscape and decidedly Low Church inhabitants. Why was he sent out there?

Mousey   Travel a lot, do you, Magda?

Chick (*to* **Magda**)   Who knows? God is everywhere, in every nook, on every stair.

Magda (*to* **Mousey**)   I travel for work. I make an uncomfortable tourist.

Mousey   We've a lovely little place on the Algarve. Mock-authentic Moorish. Yourself and Francis should come down for a bit of golf.

Magda   Thanks, but work, commitments.

Mousey   What *is* your work, Magda?

Magda   Paintings.

Mousey   Paintings what?

Magda   I sell . . . I advise . . .

Mousey   What, I tell you the colour scheme of my dining room and you find me a little piece to hang over the sideboard, is that it?

Magda   No. I look after my father's paintings.

Mousey   Your father?

Magda   Yes.

Mousey   He's famous, isn't he?

Magda   He was, for a time.

Mousey   Was?

Magda   He's dying.

Chick   Louise!

Louise   My doctor said self-expression is very good for you. Creativity is beneficial. Art is therapy.

Chick   We also have some of Louise's original lamp bases. Show them your lamps, Louise.

Louise *glares at* **Chick**.

Louise   Lamp bases were last year. I'm moving into stained glass.

Mousey   Not permanently, I hope.

Magda   Does anyone have a cigarette?

Chick /Louise   No.

Magda   I've given them up anyway. It's easier when you feel old: no effort, no premeditation. It's probably the most spontaneous thing I've ever done.

Mousey   Stop smoking?

Magda   Age. Age. I thought, I really need to stop smoking, so many people dying. I should try to stay alive, quit. And, having said that, I'd love a fag, you know?

Pause. **Magda** *seems uncomfortable, over-exposed.*

Louise (to **Magda**)   I butterflied a lamb. It's marinating. As soon as the barbecue gets going, we'll pop it on.

Chick (*to* **Mousey**)   Francis loves a butterflied lamb. He'll be beating a path to the door, won't he, Magda?

Beat.

Magda?

Magda   Will he?

Pause.

Mousey (*to* **Magda**)   Dying? Sorry to hear that.

Magda   It's not . . . It wasn't unexpected, he's been ill for some time.

Mousey   Come down the coast. Get yourself a *finca*, nice little hacienda, a pool, you're laughing.

Magda   I haven't really thought beyond the next few days.

Mousey   Messy business death, but it has its compensations.

Mousey *makes money gesture.*

Magda (*to* **Mousey**)   Is your father alive?

Mousey   No.

Chick (*almost igniting barbecue*)   Please God . . .

Magda   Your mother?

Mousey   Yes.

Magda   That's nice. That's nice for you.

Chick (*barbecue*)   Come on. Come on.

Magda   They say the world is sufficient to kill a father; a mother you have to kill with your own hands.

Chick   Goodness, Francis is late.

Mousey   No fear of that. My mother, thankfully, is a great old thing, a rock.

Louise   A rock. Is that what people want mothers to be, a rock? My mother is a rock? Rock.

Magda (*to* **Mousey**)   I lost my mother . . .

Chick .   What time is it anyway?

Louise   I lost my mother, my passport and my wedding ring.

Mousey   All at the same time?

Louise   No.

Chick   You were telling Mou . . . Brian about your courses, Louise. Louise!

Mousey   Barbecuing wasn't one of them, I take it. Ha ha!

Mousey *has made a joke he's pleased with.*

Chick   We may have to use the oven.

Mousey   Let's.

Louise   I did floristry, they said I was stiff; photography, they said I was lifeless. Media studies, macramé, vegetarian cooking for three, stencilling, women's studies, pottery, rake, printing, aromatherapy, etching, creative writing, fashion, seasonal poetry, calligraphy and heraldry. I sometimes get disillusioned, you see.

She laughs.

Chick   Louise.

Louise One hundred-plus ideas for Polyfilla – starts September. You can never tell really, till you try it.

Ominous weather sounds.

Chick Plan B, Louise. What do you think?

Louise What plan was that?

Mousey There must be a bit of an old artist in *you*, Magda. What?

Magda I don't . . .

Mousey I couldn't draw a straight line.

Magda I never wanted to.

Mousey What's that?

Magda I'm not an artist. I was an artist's daughter. It's quite a different thing.

Chick Advertising is, of course, an art form in itself. I did a lovely little campaign for a bedtime sedative recently . . .

Louise We use it all the time.

Chick Little bears in their pyjamas . . .

Louise Just back from the woods, you see. Sleepy.

Chick Very good drawings of bears. Very good, very good. You'd have liked them, Magda.

Magda I'm sure.

Mousey Magda's not interested in cartoon bears, are you, Magda?
Your type are beyond all that.

Magda Sorry?

Mousey Magda types . . .

Magda Type, what types?

Mousey My business is knowing what makes people tick.

Louise   Has anyone seen the dog?

Mousey (*to* **Magda**)   Now, in my estimation, what you and your type like are the throw-a-bit-of-paint-on-the-wall, the . . . What's her name, leave-your-messy-knickers-on-the-bed girlie?

Magda   Tracey Emin.

Louise   I would have left someone else's knickers on the bed. Chick, have you seen the dog?

Chick   Be quiet, Louise.

Mousey (*to* **Magda**)   Am I right?

Magda   I think she's . . . interesting.

Mousey (*to* **Chick**)   There. You see?

Magda   I'm not her biggest fan.

Mousey   You never had a family, of course, did you, of your own?
You and Francis?

Magda   What's that got to do with my liking or disliking modern art?

Mousey (*to* **Chick**.)   What's happening here? I'm starving.

He stands up, walks to the barbecue and peers in.

Magda   Francis can't bear the notion of fatherhood. It's what drew us to one another.
We paint a very barren landscape, Mousey.

The barbecue suddenly ignites spontaneously.

Mousey   Jesus!

Louise   Oh good, it's working.

Chick   Now. Now. You're grand. Now we're laughing. Have a drink. Louise, get Mousey, get Brian a drink /

Mousey   Christ!

Chick   Cheers.

Mousey *is given a drink.*

Chick   Where's that lamb, Louise! Now. Magda?
(*Drinking.*) Cheers, everyone! A toast to the campaign to end
campaigns.

Louise   Cheers.

Chick   Little wannabe priesties will be coming out of the
woodwork. So they will.
Cheers. Now.

Mousey (*warily*)   Cheers.

Chick   Lamb, Louise, get / the lamb.

Magda   I think, to sell someone something, you have to
make them feel lonely first, or nostalgic or deprived or lost.

Chick   Tell you, we are going to write a damn fine
campaign. Seven words. Seven little . . . Lamb, Louise.

Louise   Yeah, yeah. You couldn't really use bears for
getting priests. That would be silly.

Chick   That's right, Louise, it would be silly. Lamb.

Magda   I think you have to exploit weakness.

Louise   Maybe a different kind of animal.

Magda   *Understand* weakness.

Magda (*to* **Mousey**)   Say you're in the supermarket and
you need cat food . . .

Mousey   We don't actually keep a cat.

Magda   You need cat food. The cat reminds you of your
mother.

Mousey   Hardly . . .

Magda   You are standing by the pet food. You are rattled. All those years of batting away opportunity, you will leave no one behind. But you've got the cat. At least you have the cat, now choose the food.

Mousey   They are not my favourite / animal.

Magda   Catty Din-Dins – cheap. Catty Pretty – less cheap. Mother Love – seriously expensive. What do you go for?

Mousey (*to* **Chick**)   Are you actually expecting Francis?

Chick   Sorry, sorry about, that, he will be . . . He said he'd be / here.

Magda   Choose.

Mousey   Choose?

Magda   Catty Din-Dins, Catty Pretty, Mother Love.

Mousey   Catty Din-Dins.

Magda   Mother Love. You'd buy the cat Mother Love. You're over thirty, you have no kids, you're either sleeping with a married man or not sleeping with the man you married. Pick up Mother Love, put it in your basket. The industry knows you; this is your profile, this is who you are.

Mousey   I don't have a cat. And I am not sleeping with a man! Married or otherwise.

Chick   OK.

Mousey   People come to me, Magda, looking for expertise, not cat food.

Louise   Ask *me*.

Beat.

Magda . . .

Magda   What?

Louise   Ask me?

Magda   Ask you?

Louise   To choose.

Chick (*scratching*)   Don't.

Magda   Choose.

Louise   Mother Love. I would crawl over glass to buy Mother Love.

Mousey   Well, there we go, it's a woman thing. Women, woman. I am married to one.

Chick (*handing plate to* **Mousey**)   Here. Start with the coleslaw.

Pause. **Mousey** *takes plate and begins eating.*

Chick (*whispered pleading for lamb*)   Louise.

Louise   Hold on, I'm trying to remember a joke.

Magda   Food is the new sex.

Mousey *hands plate back to* **Chick**.

Chick   Christ, where's Francis?

Louise   I much prefer food to sex.

Magda   The world is feminised. Young men want new shoes more than sex.

Louise   Oh, I remember. What lies shivering at the bottom of the ocean? A wreck. No, no. What? What did I say?

Louise *starts to giggle.*

Chick   Nervous, you forgot . . .

Louise   A nervous wreck. You see? A nervous wreck.

Her laughter very gradually becomes hysterical.

Magda There are no men and women any more, there is just population.
A technological population, and all they need is to eat.

Louise A nervous wreck.

Magda Eating is dancing.

Chick (*to* **Mousey**) Dips?

Magda This technological population eat their way to promotion, eat their way to each other's Scandinavian beds in each other's hacienda. Eating is commerce and sex is art.

Louise Has anyone . . .

Chick I'll go and get that lamb.

Louise (*overcome with laughter*) *Has* anyone seen the dog?

Sound of thunder.

(*Laughing.*) He's lying with his head in his dish!
I thought, that's the last time I'm buying him Catty Din-Dins!
(*Almost hysterical with laughter.*) I . . . I gave my medication to the dog and he is dead.

A heavy rain begins to fall.

The dog is dead

She is in hysterics.

Mousey What the fuck is / wrong with her?

Louise I have to get the dips, dips dips, dips dips dips dips dips.

Mousey (*to* **Chick**) Do you have a campaign for me or not?

Louise *is still hysterical.*

Chick I . . . Seven words . . . seven words . . .

Louise (*to* **Mousey**, *suddenly regaining control*)   I think God took my baby back. I don't think I was enough of a rock. Does He do that, do you think? Does God take babies back if their mothers aren't rocks?

Magda   Louise / come inside . . .

Mousey   Which are?

Chick   What?

Mousey   Seven words, which are?

Louise *begins to cry.*

Magda   Chick! Come on, Louise.

Mousey   Which are?

Chick   Seven words?

Crying gets louder.

Magda   Chick!

Chick   What?

Mousey   Give me the seven fucking words.

Magda   Chick.

Mousey   Give me the words.

Chick (*clearing his throat*)   Love. Sex. Death. Faith.

Mousey   Yeah?

Chick   Love.

Mousey   You already said that.

Chick   Love . . .

Mousey   This isn't some pissy little job for a has-been. These are men of influence. These are the men on which our society was built! You were always a fuck-up, you and your girly shoes and your daddy with the wig. Is it any wonder they beat the crap out of you?

Magda   Chick.

Chick *takes* **Louise** *from* **Magda** *and holds her.*

Chick   It's just a blip, sweetheart, just a . . . I'm sorry, Mousey. I'm sorry.

He holds **Louise**, *who begins to calm down. Beat.*

Mousey (*to* **Chick**)   You've got twenty-four hours, then you're fired.

Exit **Mousey**.

Scene Two

Beach. A hospital monitor is showing arrhythmic signs of life.

Francis *is visiting Jakey.*

Francis   Well, pal. Awaiting clearance, are you? So. So so so so so so so. So? You need . . . what? Fruit? No.

Beat. Monitor bleeps.

Bleep.

Monitor bleeps twice.

Bleep. Bleep.

Beat.

You're a conversational font, I must say. I am here to pay my respects. I am here to say goodbye. Not best favourite with your daughter at the moment. She thinks I am a fool.

Beat.

So do you, you old bollox, I can tell. Your breathing has taken on a nuance of irritation.

He moves around, occasionally imitating the sound of Jakey's breathing.

I like looking out of hotel windows, that's my all-time number-one activity. I like feeling sorry for people. It is a source of comfort to me that there are so many many dull incompetent people roaming the streets, so many ordinary people.

You and I – yes, I do include myself in that little coterie, Jakey – we are a cut above the rest. Talent. Talent. She may not like it, but she knows. Let's not be too hard on her, eh?

(*Confidentially.*) I first kissed Magda by the harbour wall. She was a lamb. She said, my father is a painter – as if I didn't know. She held my hand at your exhibition. She led me past walls of naked women with big sepia tits. She led me to your *installation*. *This* is experimental, she said, *this* is a departure. She was so serious, so fucking sweet. We stepped inside. Tiny room, black box. I saw nothing. I heard your heartbeat. I distinctly remember thinking: 'This is art, and my mother would keep the coal in it.' And then, overhead, I saw him, projected on to the ceiling – a tiny man, curled like a foetus, combing his hair. A little mechanical man endlessly, absently, combing his hair. There he was, the ghost of my father that I had wiped like shit from my shoe. My little father who combed his hair before answering the telephone/

She said: 'Does he make you think of someone?' I said: 'Yes. My father.' She said: 'Was it awful when he died?' So reserved. I said no, it wasn't actually. It was disappointing. I had wanted to lose the whole fucking lot of them, in one fell swoop; something big, something gaudy.

Her delicate little face was stoical. But she should have read the signs.

The sounds from the monitor get slower. Monitor slows further.

OK, here it is: You had no fucking right to my admiration, no fucking right to my respect. Let's not beat around the bush here, Jakey, I was fucking gagging for your approval. And you shat on me, with your casual glance in the other direction, your grimace of disapproval, your stifled yawn of boredom every time I cast my shadow at your door.

Monitor stops.

No. No. No. No. No. No. Come back. I am . . . I matter . . . I am the talent . . .

See it. You fucking owe it to me. You ransacked my life. You couldn't let her go, could you?

See it. See me! See me!

(*Standing on chair, shouting at monitor.*) Bollox.

There is a long high-pitched wail from the monitor. Jakey is dead. **Francis** *stares at monitor.*

Scene Three

Beach, set up as hospital waiting room.

Magda *sits on a plastic chair. She has a mobile phone in her hand. She turns sharply as if someone has called her name. No one is there.*

Enter **Chick** *with two take-out coffees.*

Magda   Did you just call me?

Chick   No.
(*Coffee.*) Here.

Magda   Thanks. How is she?

Chick   They're adjusting her medication. Diluting her into manageable parts.

Magda   I should get back, to Jakey.

Chick   Drink your coffee

Magda   Yes. Sorry.

Beat.

Goretti, she's a nun she's a friend / she says people who are dying sometimes hold on when someone is with them. Then, you know? You might have been doing a twenty-four-hour vigil, you nip out to have a fag for five minutes and, bang, they're gone.

Beat.

They need to be alone, I suppose. To let go.

Chick   Take your time. He'll still be there.

Magda   Do you think so?

Beat.

Chick (*indicating mobile phone*)   Any word from Francis?

Magda   No.

Beat.

Do you know her, the mermaid? Did he say anything to you?

Chick   She's a waitress?

Magda   Is she?

Chick   It's nothing. She's a kid. She's / just . . .

Magda   He left me.

Chick   Why? What's different about this time?

Magda   I offended him. I told him his novel was awful.

Chick   It is awful.

Magda   Have you read it?

Chick   No.

Magda   He says he has a bigger life to lead.

Chick   Balls.

Magda   He wants to be famous. He should have married Jakey.

Chick   He wasn't pretty enough.

Magda   Jakey?

Chick   Francis.

Beat.

Magda   You're worried about Louise.

Chick   Am I?

Magda   You're shredding your coffee cup.

Chick   She's nuts, you know?

Magda *smiles. Beat.*

I met her on an aeroplane. She was wearing blue, blue jeans with daisies sewn . . . what's the word?

Magda   Embroidered?

Chick   First thing she said to me, she said the beautiful thing about aeroplanes is the lifejacket's right under your seat.

Pause.

I chose her. I chose this life.

Magda   Love.

Chick   I looked at her. I remember. I could see an outline, a tiny butterfly of cunt among the daisies. And I had the most electrifying moment of optimism.

Beat.

Love. I suppose. Yes.

Magda   Jakey said there are more potent states: lust, obsession . . .

Beat.

I didn't think he would die like this – nappies and tubes.

Pause.

I must get back / to him.

Chick What will you do?

Magda I don't know. I thought Francis . . . I thought
I'd / we'd get around to . . . I think it's too late. Do you
think it's too late?

Beat.

I've never been on my own. When my mother died I took
care of Jakey and then there was Francis and there was
never / time.

Beat.

Children. Sometimes I think of that.

Chick He'll come back. He'll always come back, Magda.

Magda You don't understand. I don't want him back.

Enter **Louise**, *buoyant, holding a scan photo.*

Louise I am a rock. They can eat their medication. Look.
I am a rock. He is embedded in me.

Louise *shows* **Chick** *the baby scan. He looks at it in disbelief.*

Chick What?

Louise I am a rock. They found him. I am a rock.

Louise I told you I was a rock. You told me I was
delusional.

Chick You poisoned the dog.

Louise Are you going to hold that against me? Look at
him.

Magda Congratulations.

She hugs **Louise**.

Congratulations, Louise. I'm glad you are a rock.

Louise Where are you going? We have to celebrate.

Magda   I need to . . . Jakey.

Louise   You tell Jakey I am a rock. Tell Jakey I am a rock.

Magda   Why, Louise?

Louise   He knows. He said: 'Louise, you are Amazonian. You are all earth.'

Magda   When did he say that to you?

Louise   One of those exhibitions. Francis brought us along. You were very pale, you didn't notice me. I was looking at a woman on the wall, big big woman, big legs, she was a giant. Jakey was behind me, he asked me what I thought of her. I said: 'You have painted my mother, my mother is a giant.' He was very pleased. I liked him. He held my face in his hands. He said: 'You are Amazonian, you are all earth.' Now. A rock. He will remember me. Tell him.

Scene Four

Louise *exercising at an antenatal class.*

Louise   My ambition was to be an air hostess and walk very fast through international airports in fifteen-denier navy-blue tights. Training was fun: sometimes we pretended the airplane had crashed and we crawled along the strip lighting without chipping our nail varnish. Then one morning I woke up and thought the world was ending. I plucked my eyebrows off, all of them, perched on the Armitage Shanks with the tweezers. I just kept going. When I went to work my instructor told me I was cosmetically unfit to fly.
I said: 'Hey, that is the least of your problems. The world is ending, which is certain to impact more on the airline industry.' They let me go. I had to give back my wheelie-bag.

You are born with all your eggs. It is predetermined how many chances one has to conceive. If I have three hundred and sixty eggs, do the maths, lose one a month from fourteen to forty-four, whatever, I'm saying you don't have as many dissolute mornings pulling spaceships full of sperm out of yourself as you think.

You think these things are symmetrical, life and death, or parallel. They are not.

And I grow now, a new person. This umbilical creature is in there unlearning everything it already knows. It has been instructed to forget its ancient genetic recipe. Of course there is mortal sin; the punishment is to be born.

I will dress it and educate it and put money in its piggy-bank and accept its food fads and buy it something genetically modified for its tea. Others being born at this very moment will be annihilated, blown apart to make face powder for the gods. It's no wonder I recarpet, discuss the extension. I am a super-fluent extension discusser. I can discuss attics, patios, conservatories, I can turn your downstairs bathroom into a giraffe house. I am fine. I have not sufficient imagination to realise the full horror. I know the safety procedures.

She silently points to the exits, front, rear and over-wing.

I love my children.

I know enough to keep my head above water. I know enough to stay afloat.

My ambition now is to be indispensable. Solid. Dependable. A tower of strength. A mountain of sense. Earth. (*Pause.*)

It's nice being married. We chop each other off at the knees.

Scene Five

Beach, as hospital in Scene Nine.

Magda *stands looking at the hospital monitor, which is silent, closed down.*

Enter **Francis**. *He waits for her to speak.*

Magda   Goretti met me at the door. She said, your daddy has gone to heaven. I didn't know who she was talking to.

Pause.

Me. She was talking to me.

Francis   I tried to find you. I went to Chick's.

Magda   I was here, we were all here, downstairs. Louise had a . . .

Francis   A what?

Magda   Episode. Louise had an episode.

Francis   Oh.

Magda   I waited with Chick. We talked.

Francis   What did you talk about?

Magda   What?

Francis   You and Chick?

Magda   I don't know. I can't remember.

Beat.

He waited to be alone. Goretti said that, she said sometimes a person won't let go until they are alone.

Francis   Right.

Magda (*pointing at body*)   Why the pillow?

Francis   They put that there to keep his jaw closed. Before, you know, his body stiffens.

Magda   Oh, right.
(*Becoming distressed, looking for things.*) A suit, I brought in a suit for him. It's here somewhere.

Francis   It's all right, they'll take care of all / that . . .

Magda   If they've mislaid it . . . It's not like he had more than one. Why a suit, for Christ's sake? I don't even know if it fits him.

Magda *breaks down.*

Francis   Shhh, Magda, come on / shh . . .

Magda   He didn't wear fucking . . . Why did they tell me to? He wasn't like them, he wasn't like them.

She cries. **Francis** *holds her.*

I didn't love him. I never loved him. Duty, fucking duty, it was all fucking duty.

Francis   You're upset. You don't know what you are talking about.

Magda   I can't breathe. I can't breathe. I can't . . .

She becomes more distressed.

Francis (*shaking her*)   Stop. Stop it, Magda.

Magda (*quietly*)   Do you think he can hear / me?

Francis   No.

Magda   Somewhere?

Francis   No.

Pause.

I'll take you home.

Magda   Tonight . . .

Francis   It's all right, I'm coming home.

Magda   Tonight. I'd be grateful if you would stay with me tonight. Then I want you to go.

Francis   What do you mean?

Magda *looks around.*

Magda   Have I forgotten anything?

Francis   I love you.

Pause. She looks at him.

Magda   Do you want to say goodbye to Jakey?

Francis   Jakey and I said our goodbyes.

Magda *turns to look at Jakey, then back to* **Francis**.

Magda   Take me home, Francis, please.

Scene Six

Beach. Swivel chair, papers blowing across the beach.

Chick   We were employed, we got the job.

We shared a chalet, my father and I, politely pouring each other's tea, our little reduced family. Between shows he'd take out his nail scissors, make paper napkins into elephants, newspapers into rows of children hand in hand. He made me a swan, which I still have.

Near the beginning of the season, the lads, the boyos who oiled the hurdy-gurdies and cleared the scum from the boating lake, the boyos who whistled at girlies whose legs were mottled with cold, those boyos . . . those boyos came to our cabin one night and called my father outside and kicked the shit out of him.

It was a hostile place, wet fields, cold beach, damp people in chair-o-planes. After our last performance of the day we would sit in the restaurant, under the glass-bottomed pool, and looked up at the boyos doggy-paddling, exuberant, the end of their shift. They kept their heads above the surface. Their Y-fronts flapped around their thighs. I'd steal my father's chips as he watched them; he wouldn't notice.

I had to admire the boyos for spotting it so fast. His tendencies. It's like I say, I was always missing the central bit, the bit that made the other bits make sense.

The poor old man. The poor sweetheart. It is why I don't believe in God. God, if He existed, would have given my father some discernment.

After they dried off with their vests, they'd come and sit near us. The boyos hissing and bending over the Formica-topped tables. We were the professionals, we didn't flinch. Once, they held my head under the water until my lungs burst and I choked on other people's chlorine and urine.

They're old men now, the boyos. Living with too much wallpaper.

They have had their own children. Their children are grown up now. Their children are optimistic boys in short-sleeved shirts and clackety-clack girls with diaphragms. Their children are sentimental about their fathers, but by Christ they never want to be them.

So this was it then: origami man in his toupee clapping his fat hands for the boys, and a mother in a blue car, gone.

I felt a knot of clarity in the rage. Later, years later, in the back seat of a motor car, my head catapulted between the thighs of a girl called June, I thought I heard him calling me. Then a readdressed letter told me he was dead. Peacefully, the letter writer, some mildewed relation, said.

A great man for tricks, she wrote, how lucky to have known him. How lucky. He disappeared; the greatest trick of all. I hear him at night, his voice a whisper in the din. I live with a ceaseless parade of activity and need. Other people's. Everybody roaring to be loved. I don't want to be touched. I don't like being touched. I don't want any fucking bonhomie.

He stands up to leave.

I have recently come to realise: every day hurts me.

Scene Seven

Beach. Bar set-up with shell stools, as in Scene Two.

Java *is working. Enter* **Francis***. Downstage,* **Mousey** *struggles to get on to bar stool.*

Francis   I've been looking for you.

Java *appears very unhappy to see* **Francis***.*

Java   Hi. Sorry.

Francis   I've missed you.

Java   Yeah?

Francis   Look, this is business. It's not going to take all night. Lets go somewhere / after

Java   I can't.

Francis   I'll wait till your shift / is

Java   It's not / it's my boyfriend. It's Matt.
Something changed. He, I, we, it's better you know, good, important. Better.

Francis   We'll talk about this later, yeah?

Java   I can't.

Francis   Matt.

Java   I'm sorry.

Francis   Jesus, Java.

Java   Look. Sex /

Francis   Yes?

Java   Sex with you made me realise that I'm really into Matt.

Beat.

Sorry.

Beat.

Francis   Right.

Beat.

Java   I'm sorry.

Beat.

Francis   Well. Glad I was of some service.

Java   We're going to have our rings blessed by his guru.

Francis   That's a humanist thing, is it?

Java   Some people find real joy in commitment.

Francis   Some people floss regularly.

Beat.

The Medoc. Two glasses.

He goes downstage to **Mousey**.

Mousey   What is this place?

Francis   Sit down.

Mousey   I'm trying to.

Francis   Concept, it's conceptual.

Mousey   What's the concept?

Francis   Fish.

Mousey   Fish?

Francis   Don't ask.

Mousey   Where's Chick? How come you guys are never in the same room at the same time?

Francis   There's only one of us.
(*Unpacking case with electronic equipment.*) Right. What is God?

Mousey   Hah?

Francis Java!
(*To* **Mousey**.) What is God?

Pause. **Mousey** *has no idea.*

God is a concept.

Mousey Fish!

Francis Fish are a concept, yes, but that's a different concept. Java!

Java What?

Francis Wine.

Java (*calling*) I heard you the first time.

Mousey I don't think she likes you.

Francis She likes me. She likes me so much it frightens her. Right. Now. What was the first thing I asked myself about this campaign?

Mousey Eh?

Francis I asked myself what. What are we selling?

Mousey The Christian Brothers.

Francis No, Mousey . . .

Mousey Brian.

Francis Bigger than that, Mousey. Much bigger than that.

Mousey Bri / an . . .

Francis We are selling God.

Mousey God?

Francis God, Mousey, is an *idea*. The big idea. The big idea for a small era. Move over, organic bananas.

Enter **Java** *with wine.*

Goodbye, Rescue Remedy. God is back and He's big.

Java   Would you like me to pour?

Francis   What's the problem, sweetheart? Feeling an attention deficit?

Francis moves to touch **Java**, *but she grabs his hand and stops him.*

Java   Don't flatter yourself. I've had more fun with scissors and glue and three empty yogurt cartons.

She goes.

Francis   See what I mean? She's all over me.

Francis turns on audio equipment.

Tape.

> **Francis**   Testing, one two, one two. Vox pop: what is God?

Francis   Listen.

Various different voices can be heard on the tape: older woman, child, young man, teenager etc. **Francis** *and* **Mousey**'s *dialogue continues under tape.*

Tape.

> **Francis**   One two, one two. OK, here we go. Research recruitment campaign.
> What is God?
>
> **Vox Pop**   God is love. He's the one true Church.
> He's in the bottom of my wardrobe.
> He's Jesus' daddy.
> He's a light. He's a light in your soul.
> He's like a total irrelevance.
> He's my reason for getting out of bed in the morning.
> Em, what?
> God? He's holy.
> He's the Father.

Francis   Clueless, right?

Mousey   Right.

Francis But we know. What do we know?

Mousey I don't know what we know.

Francis We know that God is a concept. Sit down.

Francis *plays new tape, very loud, very clear, a perfect sound with reverb.*

    Male voiceover GOD (GOD, GOD, GOD), A BIG
IDEA FOR BIG BOYS (BOYS, BOYS, BOYS).
GOD (GOD, GOD, GOD), A BIG IDEA FOR BIG
BOYS (BOYS, BOYS, BOYS).
GOD (GOD, GOD, GOD), A BIG IDEA FOR BIG
BOYS (BOYS, BOYS, BOYS).

Java *stares at* **Francis**.

Francis *(shouting)* Count them.

    Female voiceover GOD (GOD, GOD, GOD), A
BIG IDEA FOR BIG BOYS (BOYS, BOYS, BOYS).

Mousey *(shouting)* Seven. Seven.

    Female voiceover GOD (GOD, GOD, GOD), A
BIG IDEA FOR BIG BOYS (BOYS, BOYS, BOYS).

Francis Sex, Mousey. We are selling sex.
God is the new sex. The body of Christ has never been so
desirable.

Mousey Sex!

Francis Picture it. Screen-size mouth. Foreground, guys:
cool, young, cropped, pierced. They're grappling with
something, something . . . conceptual. It's in the way they
slouch. We're talking boy band meets existential anxiety.
Love, death, desire. They're searching, searching for the
meaning behind the word.

Enter **Chick**.

And now, as they say, for the science;

Female voiceover   GOD (GOD, GOD, GOD), ARE YOU BIG ENOUGH?

Francis (*whispering*)   Where the fuck were you?

Chick   Sorry. Did I miss it?

Francis   Did I . . . Yes.

Chick (*nodding towards* **Mousey**)   Like it?

Mousey   Like it? This is not a campaign. This is a concept. Again.

Francis *rewinds.*

Francis   You look like shit. What's wrong with you?

Chick   Got a call . . .

Male voiceover   GOD (GOD, GOD, GOD), A BIG IDEA . . . /

Mousey   Play him the girlie bit.

Chick   Dessie . . .

Chick *sits down, can't continue.*

Francis   Dessie what?

Female voiceover   ARE YOU BIG ENOUGH?

Mousey   Fantastic!

Francis   What? Dessie what?

Chick   Is this it? Did we write this?

Francis   Dessie what?

Chick   Blew his brains out.

Mousey   I love it. I love it.

Female voiceover   GOD (GOD, GOD, GOD), A BIG IDEA . . .

Francis   What are you talking / about?

Chick   He's dead.

Mousey   Love / this . . .

Female voiceover/Mousey . . . FOR BIG BOYS

Mousey (*imitating reverb*)   Boys boys boys boys.

Francis (*snapping*)   Turn it off.

Mousey   What? What's the problem?

Francis *turns off tape. Silence.*

Chick   He was packed up ready to come home. Bamber was bringing him home. Rest, you know? Home for a rest. He told Bamber he had a few loose ends to sort out, a few goodbyes. He drove to Wal-Mart, parked. Opened the glove compartment, took out a gun and blew his brains out. (*Quietly.*) Bang.

Pause.

Francis   Jesus.

Mousey   Who?

Francis   Dessie. Dessie.

Chick   Bamber phoned. He said, don't answer any questions, don't answer the telephone.

Mousey   Get him a drink.

Francis   Java!

Mousey   Get him a drink, for fuck's sake.

Francis   Java! Java.

Chick   He was all packed, you know, ready to go. Made his bed, Bamber said. He'd even made the bed. Why would you make the bed if you . . .

Java *arrives.*

Java   What?

Mousey   Jesus.

Java   What?

Francis   Brandy. Bring the bottle.

Java *goes to get drink. Silence.*

Chick   You, eh, you like the concept then, Mousey?

Mousey   Terrific. Knew it would be.

Java *returns.*

Java   Celebrating, are we?

Francis   No.

Mousey   When it comes to God, to selling God and that, you're the boyos. You guys know the territory.

Chick   We're the boyos all right.

Silence. **Mousey** *and* **Francis** *watch* **Chick**.

Java   What is up with you guys?

Francis *begins filling glasses.*

Francis (*to* **Java**)   Sit down.

Chick   My brother / he . . .

Java   Your brother the rabbit?

Mousey (*to* **Francis**)   Who's a rabbit?

Chick   He shot himself.

Francis (*to* **Mousey**)   Just shut it . . .

Mousey (*to* **Francis**)   Hey, cool it.

Java (*to* **Chick**)   The rabbit shot himself?

Chick   Yes.

Java   Oh.

Mousey (*to* **Chick**)   What do you mean, he was a rabbit? (*To* **Francis**.) I was never told Dessie was a rabbit. (*To* **Chick**.) Why wasn't I told Dessie was a rabbit?

Francis (*to* **Mousey**)   I thought I told you to shut the fuck up.

Java (*to* **Chick**)   Why?

Chick   I think he was very lonely.

Mousey (*to* **Francis**)   Look. It is my business to know if people turn themselves into rabbits. It could have some serious implications for my client relation / ship.

Java   That's really sad.

Mousey   Messy. It's very messy, very very messy, badly handled. Should never have let it get that messy.

Francis   Sue the fuckers. Sue the Brothers. Sue them. What did they think they were doing, sending the poor bastard to Iowa? He should have been . . . He had problems . . . He needed . . . I don't fucking know. Sue them.

Mousey   What are you talking about, sue them? He shot himself. He didn't choke on his communion wafer.

Java   Was he wearing his bunny suit when he died?

Beat.

Chick   I don't know, Java. They didn't tell me that.

Java   It would be hard to shoot yourself in a bunny suit because you would have paws.

Francis *glares at her.*

Chick   He had no one, had he? Me. Christ.

Francis   It's the loneliest job in the world. He might as well have been a fucking astronaut.

Mousey   Lookit. Lookit. We're taking our eye off the ball. This is a fucking great campaign. Dessie would be proud of you, Chick, if he could see this campaign. Making this the best fucking recruitment campaign ever is your memorial to Des. To a life of worship and self-sacrifice. To a life of dedication.

Beat. Suddenly **Francis** *lunges at* **Mousey** *and hits him. There is a scuffle.*

Francis   Shut up! Shut the fuck up! You slimy piece of shit.

Mousey   You, you . . .

Francis   It's a horrendous campaign. It's a travesty. It cheapens me to even have to think about those bastards and all the fuckwits they spawned.

Mousey   What are you talking about? You'd be nothing without them. None of us. Little Chickalatta here with his poofy da, you with your arty-fuckin'-farty up-your-own-hole in Armani. You'd be nothing without them. Nothing.

Francis   It has taken me twenty years to wipe their shit from my shoes.

Chick   Lads. Lads.

Pause. There is a stand-off between **Mousey** *and* **Francis**.

Francis   I want to get drunk.
(*Holding* **Chick**.) Java, any self-respecting humanist would make sure this man was drunk

Java *pours.*

Francis   More.

Java (*to* **Chick**)   I'm sorry. I'm sorry about your brother. There's probably a lesson there for all of us.

Chick   Yes. Yes, there probably is.

Java   You should plant him a tree. A really good tree, that endures.

Francis (*raising his glass*)   Dessie.

All   Dessie.

Beat.

Chick   The weird thing is . . .

He begins to cry.

. . . things are looking up, you know? Things are looking up.

Scene Eight

Beach. Upstage, a small beach house/studio is visible. Beach candles around stage.

Magda *sits on sand looking out to sea.*

Magda   My mother had known all along.

I watched her dress. There was her red skirt we shook out. There was lanolin on her hands that stained. There was her lipstick. There were her shoes, her beautiful shoes, with long leather thongs that criss-crossed her legs like a warrior. All those nights our little tree pushed through the floor. We will go, she said, we will take Ozzie up on his invitation.

They were there, my father and his lover, spread over Ozzie's stormy conservatory, waiting for their drinks, watching the sea sweep over the harbour wall. The lover's husband, at the bar, seemed pleased to see us. Defeated, he was beyond outrage.

When he first met her, my father instructed her not to go to America but to stand still and be painted. She obeyed, figuring America wasn't going anywhere but my father might. He painted her in jungles, in public greenhouses, next to palms and fronds under leaves the size of umbrellas. She was, he said, Amazonian, she was all earth.

In Ozzie's conservatory, my father does not move the arm that lies on the lover's thigh, or the bare foot by her ankle.

He is in a cooler country now, a country so cold he doesn't even need expression.

They drank, the four of them. I watched. I watched the lovers' barbarism when her husband failed to entertain; I watched my mother, leaning in to my father and my father swatting her away like a fly.

I fell asleep on one of Ozzie's damp cushions, and when I woke up she was gone.

It was more than a day. The storm passed, they dredged the harbour. She was still attached, they said, the thong of her leather sandal wrapped around the gas.

Beat. Louis Armstrong's 'Mac the Knife' begins under remaining speech.

Her car was white. Driving to the hotel that night we had turned on the radio, hoping for some familiar tune. The man said: 'Louis Armstrong is dead.' And my mother cried, and I watched her, her face like a great plate of tears.

I wondered who he was.

Pause. Song continues, getting quieter. **Francis**, **Louise** *and* **Chick** *come on stage, extinguish candles. Conversation is at a low level. They are clearing up after the dispersal of Jakey's ashes. Evening darkens.*

Chick 'I saw three ships go sailing by / Over the sea, the lifting sea, / And the wind rose in the morning sky, / And one was rigged for a long journey.'

Louise I want my ashes on the mantelpiece.

Magda His instructions were very specific. Unfortunately, when her time comes, he wants me to do the same with the dog.

Louise You're sure he's gone?

Magda Sure.

Louise　You don't want bits of him washing up in rock pools, frightening small children.

Magda　He's out beyond the Kish by now.

Louise　Is the dog upset?

Magda　Like most widows, tired and over-emotional.

Louise　I'll take her.

Chick　Louise / no.

Francis　Didn't you poison your own?

Louise　No. I gave it a couple of tranquillisers.

Francis　And now it's dead.

Louise　Yes.

Francis　I rest my case. Anyway, the dog's mine. Isn't it?

Magda　I won't battle you for custody.

Louise　We need a dog. Chick wants to move to the country.

Francis　Is that another tragic misconception, Louise?

Louise　No.
I'd rather eat the cat lit, but Chick's gone all pastoral since Dessie's little accident.

Chick　It wasn't an accident, Louise.

Louise　Suicide.

Francis　It's dark in the country.

Louise　And full of sheep.

Francis　Is this true?

Chick　Yep. The MD called me in after his snowboarding trip. I helped him into his chair, he fired me. Or at least I think he did. It's difficult to tell, his voice is breaking.

Francis　Why did he fire you?

Chick Apparently I failed to ignite.

Francis So much for your bijou office on the square. Any word from Mousey?

Chick He's going with the assault course. He's going with the metaphor.

Francis Hah?

Chick Boys jumping into lakes, that sort of thing. Art, it's black and white.

Francis Art, is it? Oh well, fuck that.

Chick Imagine, we could have single-handedly revived the fortunes of the Christian Brothers. What a crucifying thought that would be to live with.

Louise (*to* **Francis**) Do you want to see a photo of our baby?

Francis No.

Louise Its little kidneys, its little spleen?

Magda What will you do in the country?

Chick Gardening? Maybe?

Francis (*looking at scan photo*) Impressive.

Chick Topiary? Pottery?

Francis It's a boy.

Louise How can you tell?

Francis There.

Louise That's the umbilical cord.

Francis Right. Right. Thank goodness for that.

Chick *moves to* **Magda**, *who is looking out to sea.*

Magda That seal keeps coming in, lifting his head to look at me.

Beat.

He expects something from me. I don't know what.
(*To the seal.*) What? What do you want?

Francis *and* **Louise** *join them downstage.*

Francis   Do you know anything about topiary?

Chick   About as much as you know about novel writing.

Magda (*watching seal*)   What does he want?

Francis   Actually, I'm writing a screenplay.

Magda   Christ.

Francis   Magda?

Magda   It's nothing to do with me any more.

Francis (*to* **Chick**)   I'm being left. It's not official. We
haven't torn the photographs in half.

Louise   I would have left you years ago.

Magda   You can have the photographs. They're all of you
anyway. (*To* **Chick**.) I'm going to live in Jakey's studio. I
like it, you can see the harbour.

Francis   You won't leave me, Magda.

Magda   No?

Louise   There he is. He's back.

Pause. They all look at the seal.

Do we do something? Some gesture or something?

Magda *stands up and walks towards the shore. A strip of light like a
runway becomes apparent. The stage dims as if we are being carried
away from it by the sea.*

Magda   We said goodbye, Jakey. I carried you to the sea,
Jakey, and the sea lit up like a runway.

Go.
Go on, Jakey. It's time to go now.

They leave the stage carrying candles, etc., low conversation continuing among them.